Forty Years a Guinea Pig

DEDICATED TO—

My grandfather—Dr. John Samuel Morrow
My parents—Reverend John Eugene and Mary Hayes Morrow
My wife—Catherine Gordon Morrow
My sister—Nellie Katherine Parker
My brothers—John H. Morrow, William H. Morrow, A. Eugene Morrow

Forty Years a Guinea Pig

E. Frederic Morrow

The Pilgrim Press ● New York

Library of Congress Cataloging in Publication Data

Morrow, Everett Frederic, 1909–
    Forty years a guinea pig.

    1.   Morrow, Everett Frederic, 1909–   2.   Afro-
Americans—Civil rights.   3.   Afro-Americans—
Biography.   I.   Title.
E185.97.M88A3   973'.0496073 [B]   80-16657
ISBN · 0-8298-0399-8

THE PILGRIM PRESS
132 West 31 Street
New York, New York 10001

NOTE OF ACKNOWLEDGMENT

Among those who so generously gave me the benefit of their advice and assistance in preparing this book, I would particularly like to thank Norma Salt, Harriet and Alfred Moeller, Nora Kennington, and Susan Mains. And to Esther Cohen, my editor, for her skilled professional services in organizing and editing my material.

—E.F.M.

TO BE BLACK, TO BE LOST . . .

Ask night how it feels to be dark,
to be pitch, to be black, to be lost . . .
ask winter the feeling of cold,
the bitter edge of frost.

Ask day how it feels to be light
exposed so that all may see
through the sharp lens of the sun
the glare of intensity.

With fears that torture the dark
and days that are rimmed with pride,
ask me how it feels to be both
exposed and doubly denied.

Hannah Kahn

Foreword

I lived this story. If this were the reporting of the life of an American white, it would merely be a recording of the natural progression of a person's life from youth to old age. What makes the difference in this instance is the revealing of the infernal and everlasting structured obstacles of racism placed in the pathway of a Black who is trying to achieve within "the system."

It is difficult for a white person to understand and perceive what happens to a Black person who is competing in a white American culture for recognition and identity and a sense of worth. Even after three hundred years of living in America, the insidious effects of slavery still remain, even though slave-holding was abolished over one hundred years ago. Americans may have freed their consciences by the abolition of slave-holding, but not their minds!

So many white Americans have been deceived by the passage of civil rights bills in the past twenty-five years, the not too successful efforts to integrate schools, and the feeble attempts at fair employment practices that they believe the crippling social, political, and economic shackles no longer obtain. This is a cruel myth. Despite all the hurrahs, so little has changed. To the naive, there may appear to be external signs of great progress but "the American heritage of racism" still impedes most Blacks who try to escape anonymity.

My life embraces the years when the Ku Klux Klan and White Citizens Councils were in vogue, and fair employment practices and equal opportunity employers and school busing had not been born. Any Black person who aspired to achieve a role and a life outside the laboring or domestic fields had to accept the rigors of deception, discrimination, segregation, and persecution.

My adult life as "a guinea pig" in American industry and government inspired this book. I want recent generations, Black and white, to know the genesis of some of today's accomplishments that are heralded as significant and monumental "breakthroughs" in American life. These hailed accomplishments should be measured against the sacrifices and plight of the pioneers who charted the course, mapless, friendless, and unsung.

This book is written in the hope of focusing attention on the millions of Blacks who will never get to the starting line toward a better life because of the inflexible customs in American life that ignore, and thereby endorse, the curse of color, caste, and class.

Chapter One

The office where I sit in the Bank of America International in New York's financial district is spacious and distinctive and commanding. Its furnishings give mute testimony to the fact that the bank is the world's biggest and richest, and the whirr and stir outside my office are the "human wheels" engaged in operations that will add more billions to the balance sheet by the end of the year.

I came here nearly ten years ago, as I had gone to several other jobs in the course of my life, to be a "first," a Black first. It was in the period of the Sixties when American Blacks were emerging from their cocoon of lethargic despair and self-doubt and, by fire and blood, demanding a place in American life. Cities were burning and mobs were rioting, and a new and fearless militancy had erupted in the Black ghettos of America. Stokely Carmichael was shouting "Black Power" and the Black Panthers were meeting police and national guardsmen head-on as they tried to wrest from white America civil rights, jobs, and respect.

Many of the corporate giants had been shaken to their foundations by this Black assault upon the status quo in America. The Black rabble were outside their massive doors shouting, demanding, and picketing and would not go away. They wanted "in" and until they saw some tangible evidence that corporate directors had heard and acted in response, they were going to stay in front of those doors. The Bank of America represented corporate omnipotence. It was a favorite target and to get the Bank of America to open its doors to employment of ignored minorities would be to get the message to every corporate boardroom in the country.

My employment by the bank was recommended by Robert Anderson, former Secretary of the Treasury in the Eisenhower Administration, now head of his own financial enterprise in New York and an advisory board member of the Bank of America. The wheels were set in motion, and there were weeks and weeks of letters and interviews as various and sundry bank officers "sized me up." After about two months of this, it was apparent that no one wanted to take responsibility for hiring me and each interviewer passed on the decision to someone else. I finally tired of this foot-dragging and called an official in the New York office and told him they could drop the whole idea. However, a return call informed me that there was only one more item to be taken care of and would Mrs. Morrow and I be luncheon guests of the chief executive officer in his dining room at the bank.

Catherine and I, old hands at this kind of tactic, knew what the luncheon was all about: we were to be exposed to a social situation and our manners and conversation tested to see if they met the standards of "big business" requirements. During our years in Washington we had undergone this test in the White House, in embassies, and on many trips around the world on government business. We cherished the opportunity to confound our hosts and their fearful guests.

On the day of the luncheon at the bank, Catherine, with her grace and savoir faire, charmed our host into embarrassment. Halfway through the meal he confessed why we were there:

they had to see if we "knew the ropes;" that is, how to handle the intricacies of a formal meal and participate with ease in the usual social chit-chat.

The next day the president of the bank flew in from California and accepted me into the ranks. Because of my education and background, I could have been named a vice president at the outset. However, as I was frankly told, it was felt better to start me out as an assistant vice president to avoid any possible outcry from the staff of charges of favoritism before I won my spurs by demonstration of ability.

My entry into the official family was a chilly affair. The officers were coldly polite, and the wide press coverage I got all over the country did not help. For a white man this event would have been a natural step in his working career, but for a Black it was sensational and historic, for he was breaching a heretofore invulnerable wall.

At my interview with him, the president outlined the possibilities inherent in my employment. He suggested that the bank was not interested in my becoming an ordinary factotum so there was no need to take the primary training courses given inexperienced new employees. He envisioned for me a role akin to that of a roving international ambassador, seeing my acquaintanceships with leaders throughout the world as an indispensable ingredient in the bank's determination to expand internationally. My six years in the White House and many years of activity with the permanent representatives to the United Nations gave me entree to international leaders and heads of state. This could pay off handsomely in the bank's international efforts.

This was a beautiful dream that never happened. Those in middle management have a way of destroying the plans and intentions decided upon at the highest levels of command. They can sabotage these plans in a thousand ways and top management often does not discover what went wrong. Through the years I have seen how rancor and hatred, discrimination, and fear, can hamstring Blacks in their drive toward a successful career in a giant corporation. I suppose many whites often meet these same barriers and frustrations. The difference is that not every white does.

I had watched the way personnel had brought Blacks and Hispanics into the bank at lower levels and let them stagnate and drown in punch-machine or other less imaginative jobs. Now I knew I had come to the end of an era. Until now my life had been free of compromise or knuckling under to edicts from a higher echelon that eroded my authority or lessened my influence. For more than forty years of employment in many arenas of American life I had fearlessly fought the high and the low on any issue that smacked of unfairness, discrimination, or racism. But now, I saw, I was not resisting as hard or protesting as loudly. My resentment at the efforts of mediocre men to dilute my authority and my influence did not send my temperature soaring and my voice roaring as of old. My tired mind and body told me that I had "paid my dues" and that it was time to retire and leave the roar of battle to new and younger contestants. It was this decision that sent my mind scanning the sixty-plus years of my life and the events that comprise its story.

At the outset I had naively believed that I would be extremely happy at the bank because of the reasons behind its origin. The Bank of America had been born out of the bias and discrimination directed against the immigrant Italian working class in California at the turn of the century. Tired of the upstaging and insults received from big banks in San Francisco, the illustrious founder, Amadeo Pietro Giannini, turned his genius to banking to help his discouraged and harassed compatriots. Thus, at the outset, the bank catered to the poor and deprived and developed an enviable reputation for fair play and concern for working people. During Giannini's lifetime this spirit remained intact. The bank on its way to becoming the greatest private financial institution in the world forgot its beginnings!

I officially became an officer on July 1, 1964. It was a signal occasion for me because it marked another "first," and I was determined that the probationary period would be short and successful. The great metropolitan newspapers of the country carried the story on their financial pages, and *The New York Times* featured my picture and a lengthy biographical sketch. Friends in Europe and Africa wrote that they had seen the story in papers there.

4

In the succeeding decade I participated in many areas of banking. My full vice presidency was voted by the board after three years and in 1969 I was made a division head. My duties included representing the bank on boards and in activities where a good corporate image was important. I renewed my travel to various parts of the world and held membership on an international board for educational development in the Caribbean.

From the beginning there was an undercurrent of jealousy and pique. Tom Coughran, the chief executive officer in New York, warned me that this would occur. Frequent mention of my name in the press because of my service in the two Eisenhower administrations and my current activities was not received kindly by all my associates. My frequent trips to California to the mother bank and visits to branches and assistance on urban problems all served to give too much exposure to the Black senior officer.

The kinds of slights received from fellow officers were childish and silly and they were irritating and vexing. For example, several of us rode the Wall Street express bus every day and it furnished the backdrop for a display of unfriendliness by two or three officers. Because I lived uptown, I boarded the downtown bus early and was aboard when my colleagues boarded. When they got on, they avoided seeing me and would stalk to the back of the bus without speaking. Then, to avoid walking to the office with me, they would get off before the stop nearest to the bank. Others, meeting me on the street, would suddenly look up at the sky or cross the street or look into shop windows. If accompanied by their wives, they were rude. This is conduct of the socially insecure. They are afraid to initiate or be a part of any social recognition of Blacks for fear of the diminution of their presumed higher status in the eyes of other white observers. My wife and I asked Mr. Coughran not to invite us to office parties. What made the practice of ignoring me on the outside so damnably obvious was that these same men and women when inside the bank always feigned good fellowship and mutual interests. They were hypocrites. I learned to be coldly civil and correct.

Although it was not part of my job, it was inevitable that I was drawn into early stages of integrating Blacks. During the

5

Martin Luther King period of civil rights, many corporations made a gesture toward hiring Blacks on a quota basis. Many were hired in a flush of remorse for past sins without regard to future assimilation, promotion, or even retention. Many failed but those who persevered and hung on had myriad problems. I became the "father confessor" for scores of harassed men and women, white as well as Black, who felt that my record of achievement qualified me to be their defender on the issue of equal opportunity and fair play.

Through the years at the Bank of America until he retired in 1971, Tom Coughran tried to get the managing officials in San Francisco to implement the plans which had been outlined to me in 1964. They demurred and demurred so nothing ever happened. As the years passed and my full potential was never used, I became bitter green around the edges of my soul. I had a good job and national respect but the signs were there for me to read. I had come in at fifty to put out a fire. Now calm and peace prevailed and minorities were around (in greater numbers if not in higher positions).

This stint in the financial jungle of Wall Street gave me a lesson in the philosophy of ruling white Americans that no other situation could ever have taught me. In the big corporations of America, Black executives, even senior ones, *can be in it but not of it.* They can be listed on official stationery, have stock options, executive privileges, and even a top salary, but not be present when the vital policy decisions are agreed upon or share in the intimate social gatherings where the whispered decisions that change the shape of the world are made. Boardrooms and offices are not the only meeting places where corporate strategies are developed, promotions decided, and the future shaped. These decisions are often done at posh clubs (golf or social), or on yachts or at the exclusive playgrounds of the rich that are off limits to dark skins and accents and certain designated nationalities. Blacks are not *of* these scenes no matter what their corporate designation. They cannot defend themselves against determinations that exclude them from the race to the summit!

Why have I stayed? Where could one go that would be better at this late day? Frankly, I remained hopeful that there would be change. And remaining had a certain nuisance value. Besides, as a pioneer in a field that had just opened to Blacks, I had to remember that pioneers seldom achieve the ultimate, but they do carve a path that marks the way for those who follow. My story in retrospect follows.

Chapter Two

My birth on April 20, 1909, in Hackensack, New Jersey, caused no dancing in the streets, ringing of bells, or proclamation from the mayor. The event upset the economic balance of my family and caused my father to petition the Almighty for health and strength to cope with the problems of the new arrival.

Hackensack as a small urban community offered for a Black child none of the joys of growing up which are usually associated with such communities of that era. Even though New York was just across the Hudson River, it did not change the rural unsophistication of Hackensack's inhabitants. New Jersey, as an agricultural state with its southern exposure to Delaware and its large slave population before Emancipation, promoted an atmosphere and a social structure that established Blacks as inferior.

Unlike the southern states, New Jersey seldom had signs in public places designating what was open or available to people on the basis of race, but the system employed was so ingrained and so well established by custom that signs were not necessary. In South Jersey the schools and churches, theaters, hotels, and communities were rigidly segregated by race. Blacks who went to Atlantic City or Asbury Park for a holiday, stayed in a Black hotel or rooming house, swam in a designated section of the beach called "The Ink Well," and sat in the section reserved for Blacks in one of the little joints. It was a debilitating, defeating experience, and after a few years the effects of living in this kind of atmosphere dulled the ambition and aspirations of all but a few hardy souls.

Recently my wife and I were house-hunting in Princeton. We were distressed to find in this beautiful university town the decadence of the Dutch settlers who introduced slavery to this hemisphere three centuries ago. Their misreading of life still prevails in the vestiges of racism, class, and caste that is the unwritten law. Even the local Blacks are suspicious of Black newcomers who are unwilling to subscribe to the mores and customs which were already established in town before the First Continental Congress convened in Old Nassau Hall.

It does not take a high I.Q. to imagine what it meant to grow up Black in New Jersey in the Twenties and Thirties. With every recreational, social, and economic avenue closed to Black kids and the conspiracy in the school system to give them an inferior education by relegating them to "special classes," a Black child's horizon was in the dust of the street.

My life has spanned the most dynamic and productive periods of Black development in America. I have watched my race truly come "out from the gloomy past, 'til now we stand at last, where the white gleam of our bright start is cast . . ." to quote James Weldon Johnson's "Lift Every Voice and Sing." To one not a Black, this statement is difficult to grasp. But to awaken every day with the knowledge that before it closes you will be insulted, perhaps assaulted, jailed, or slain is to live in an atmosphere that kills the spirit, stifles initiative and destroys ambition; or develops the hard-won rewards of courage and determination. The few of my generation who escaped the devastating ravages of those days have fascinating stories to tell.

This observation applies to my own life, but I am sad and

indignant about boyhood friends and acquaintances who never made it to the starting line. Black childhood in New Jersey in this period was worse than in the South because the rules were more treacherous and dishonest. There were no signs, only customs and practices which were effective and efficient. To the uninitiated, to be insulted because you did not know the custom was worse than the hard mental slap of reading a sign that shouted it loud and clear. This was every Black child's experience.

Ours was a closely knit family and we were taught to share each other's burdens, and triumphs. The axis of the family was our devoted and loving father who practiced every day the tenets and teachings of the Bible which he so faithfully and movingly preached to his congregation every Sunday morning.

My parents gave their children love and care and an example by which to live. They gave us a happy home, high educational goals to work toward, and a code to live by that denied that a Black should accept the confines of a second-class citizenship. My father's moral strength was legend in our town and he fought the fight and kept the faith, giving to all around him the aspiration to walk the world in dignity and in peace. We believed in God because we had witnessed God's work. As we struggled out of the mire of discrimination and segregation at every critical point God raised up someone to help us, just as father said would be the case.

My father died one cold day in February, 1934. He had suffered for years from a stomach ailment induced by a kick from an unruly horse in his youth. He was stricken at midnight and rushed to the hospital in an unconscious state. The doctors said he would not rally and that he was technically dead. The family remained steadfastly by his bed hoping that he might open his eyes once more and—glory be to God—a miracle occurred that startled the doctors and nurses. Father opened his eyes and smiled at us. He started singing the old spiritual "Swing Low Sweet Chariot," and we joined in. He took my mother's hand and said: "Mamie, dear, we have been as one for over forty-five years, so you know my thoughts and prayers at this time." And then his eyes went around the room and to each of his five children he gave a benediction and a "God bless you, dear." To me he said: "Son, you've been a good and responsible man and I am leaving your mother and your sister in your care. Never let them down . . ." He sang another bar of the spiritual, closed his eyes, and died.

It took us a long time to recover from this loss. His death scene was unreal but true to father's style. He brought God into that hospital room for us to behold before he crossed the bar. He left us a legacy greater than gold or silver or fame. He left us faith and courage, an honorable name, and a challenge to live by.

At twenty-five I became the head of the family with all the responsibilities and anxietites that title confers. It was the depth of the Great Depression. My father's death worsened mother's disability and she was morose, anxious, and discouraged. She feared she would be a burden to her children. However, the spirit of John Eugene Morrow lived on and armed with his motto, "Trust in God and follow his teachings, and he will have someone open a door for you," all five of his children made it.

Our mother lived another twenty years after father's death, and she glowed with pride over her children's accomplishments. She lived long enough to see the community acclaim her daughter, Nellie, the first Black school teacher in northern New Jersey. Her son John became a distinguished college professor and linguist. William became a career Army officer. In an earlier publication I made this observation about my parents: "Through my adult years the one human quality of John Eugene and Mary Anne Morrow that has impressed me most and gripped my imagination was their courage. Their relentless plodding toward a goal set for their children was contrary to all common judgment with no similar examples about them to suggest any success. In the midst of poverty and resistance, discrimination and segregation, mores and common customs, decrees and de facto preachments of Black inferiority, to be able to believe that 'God will raise up someone to act at the proper time' takes uncommon and guileless courage!" Our parents realized that if their children were to escape the road to drudgery and nothingness that began inside the

Black ghetto, it had to be by our heads and not our feet, so emphasis was concentrated on culture and education.

All of us have worn the family name proudly, and we hope to pass on to future generations of Morrows the family motto first enunciated by the patriarch, Dr. John Samuel Morrow, our paternal grandfather. John Samuel was born a slave. He was the same age as his master's youngest son, and he became a playmate and constant companion of the little white boy. This young slave was taught Latin and Greek and mathematics by his playmate's Oxford tutor and, thus, at an early age tasted the fruits of education and knowledge. He later became a distinguished minister and teacher and was driven out of North Carolina by the Ku Klux Klan for teaching former slaves to read and write. Old John Samuel in a letter to our father in the Thirties wrote: "No matter how great the problems and the obstacles confronting you and your little band, you must continue to keep on keeping on." Our parents stenciled those words on our hearts and minds at an early age . . . "to keep on keeping on!" This we all have done!

Chapter Three

I entered Bowdoin College in 1926 on a "fluke." In those days all New England colleges had an unwritten rule on minority quotas. When I applied, the admissions officer, Professor Charles Burnett, had been a classmate at Amherst of the Honorable Dwight Morrow of the class of 1893. Morrow, a nationally prominent lawyer and financier, was a senior partner of the Wall Street banking firm of J.P. Morgan. He was a power in international financial circles and in the National Republican Party. He lived on his vast estate in Englewood and I only three miles away in a very tiny home. Somehow admissions officer Burnett, in reviewing my application, took it for granted that I was a member of his old classmate's clan. He had visions of great endowments and other handsome gifts for the college, and admitted me without checking race, color, financial condition, or mental capacity. Bowdoin, anxious to make a good impression on the "scion" of Dwight Morrow, apparently alerted the fraternities and athletic team captains that I would be arriving on the "State of Maine Express" at 8:00 A.M., Monday, September 8, 1926. When the "State of Maine" puffed into the sleepy Brunswick station that morning, the platform was alive with young men, many in white sweaters with big black B's on them, indicating "letter men" from the varsity athletic teams. They were lining the platform, yelling "Hey, Morrow, hey, Morrow!"

As scores of youths loaded down with baggage emerged from the train, each was asked if he were the sought-after Fred Morrow. I was the last person to leave the train. No one asked me who I was. They all knew I could not possibly be the rich man's son for whom they were looking and ready to adore. I remember one hulking athlete saying, "I guess he didn't make this one."

I went directly from the station to the campus seeking the bursar's office. Inside my suit jacket was pinned the money for the first half-year's tuition and room. It represented thousands of hours of sweat and sacrifice by my family and me. My contribution had come from cutting lawns for the rich until I coughed up grass. To lose or misplace this small fortune would mean unprecedented and eternal calamity.

The bursar's office was a madhouse. It was small, and the main clerk on duty, a maiden lady, was harassed, tired, and out of sorts. When my turn at the window finally came, she shouted, "Go away. You were here yesterday and had your chance. Now beat it!" For a moment I thought this lady was definitely balmy. I'd never seen her before, nor she me, but her adamant attitude made me beat a hasty retreat to consider my next step. I parked bags in a corner and walked outside to get my bearings. Coming toward me was a fine-looking, smiling Black youth. What had been a mystery solved itself in a flash: this chap was the one Miss Hayes had seen 'yesterday,' and true to the old cliché that "all Blacks look alike," she had chased me away. The young stranger approached me with a smile and an outstretched hand, and said, "I'm Bill Dean. Who are you?" I told Bill my story and he nearly fell over laughing. True to my theory, he was supposed to be the token black at Bowdoin for that period, but good old Professor

Burnett's mistake had brought another one to the campus, much to the joy of both of us.

Dean and I had much in common. Our fathers were ministers. Our families had been involved in teaching and preaching to Blacks for two generations. We liked competing against odds, and we accepted with relish the challenge of being Black in a white world. We became roommates and instant friends.

The Black youths in the white colleges of America today are going through the phase of having to have a "Black Center," or Black dormitories or a "Black House," where they can lead comfortable, segregated lives and "get themselves together." I despise this practice. It robs Blacks of the opportunity to get the most out of college by denying them access to the minds, companionship, and friendship of their white classmates. It also denies them the opportunity of preparing for life by learning to understand the foibles, thinking, and philosophy of their peers who eventually will run the economic, business, and political life of our nation. This self-imposed segregation also prevents the whites from getting a full and sound education in the realities of living together in a multiracial country and world. Hence both sides lose, the Blacks most of all. Admittedly, living within an integrated system is tough. Such a scheme demands constant competition and struggle. But if you would be a champion, you must learn to compete with the challengers. Competition is the only road to excellence and acceptance, and to avoid it at any stage of one's development is to go down the road to mediocrity and anonymity.

Bill Dean and I roomed together at Bowdoin because it was cheaper to share a suite than to room alone. Also, no white picked either of us for a roommate. However, we did not become recluses and remain alone and aloof. We each had different tastes in sports, elective courses, and selection of friends. Bill was a serious student with little time for outside activities. He wanted to be Phi Beta Kappa and an honor student, so he studied night and day for this purpose. We did play tennis, go to the movies, and eat at the same boarding-house. While the whites didn't "embrace" us, they knew us and we knew them, and we got a valuable education in the frailties and philosophy of our classmates.

Bowdoin is isolated from the big cities and urban centers in the Northeast. In the long cold winters studying and learning is the primary occupation of many students. The pursuit of excellence in learning is serious. We had house parties, visiting celebrities in the fields of music, art, science, politics, and world affairs. We had concerts, winter sports, inter-collegiate debates and forums. We had "bull sessions" and beer and pretzel parties in the dormitories. Bowdoin became coeducational a few years ago, but in my day it was for men only. Minorities did not belong to the fraternities, hence our social life was almost nil. Dean and I never invited a girl to the campus because there wasn't any place to go or to entertain. Open dating of white girls was verboten—by custom and fiat. We used our leisure time to muse upon and study the practices, attitudes, and actions of our classmates, and determine methods to survive with honor in a white world.

In the last five years, I've had many young Blacks come to my office in Wall Street seeking advice on how to cope with the riddle of survival in the big corporations of America. Many had ignored the opportunity in college to study the thinking, philosophy, and attitudes of their white classmates, who were now their competitors and antagonists in the hurly-burly of corporate life. Some were intimidated, and despite good minds and fine character, they would never leave the starting line of their new careers.

In my days at Bowdoin there were only two Blacks, and in all the New England colleges at that time no more than a dozen. Out of these twelve, seven made Phi Beta Kappa and eight graduated magna or summa cum laude. Most were the products of Black high schools, and they had prepped under dedicated teachers. They asked no quarter and gave none, and they resented and fought any semblance of discrimination and segregation. They wanted to live in, eat in, participate in, and sit in integrated dormitories and classrooms, and they spent the early part of their adult lives striving to dignify and capitalize the noun "Negro."

Acceptance is something else. A Black may be shunned and ignored and even harassed by some of his white classmates. He will even encounter prejudiced professors and deans. However, this is experiencing how it really is in the normal work-a-day life of our nation. Learning how to cope with it is learning how to achieve one's goals. One must make oneself available to those who want to extend the right hand of fellowship and ignore with dignified pride and self-assurance those who do not.

Bowdoin was the greatest intellectual and social challenge I have ever known. True to its sacred hymn, it was "the nurturer of men . . ." Its fetish for excellence as a trademark sought after by all her sons, and its tutorial system and famed and dedicated professors made the system work.

My father had a philosophy that if one is decent and honest and tries his level best on all occasions to persevere toward a worthwhile goal, when he is blocked or thwarted "God will raise up someone to open the way." I have made it through sixty-five years holding tight to that truth. It has worked for me and my family all our lives. It worked at Bowdoin during the first bewildering months of our freshman year. Bill Dean and I were not instant successes, nor completely accepted by faculty and fellow students. It was a tedious effort—day in, day out—to survive, academically and socially.

One night early in the first term, when we had just received the results of the monthly hour exams, we were at a low ebb. We were in a cold, alien land, and we wondered if we were wise in our selection of this stiff, uncompromising place. When we returned from dinner there was a note under the door from our English professor, Herbert Brown, inviting us to come to his home that night for a "bull session." That evening with Herbie Brown was a landmark in our lives. He gave us the greatest pep talk we had ever had, and challenged us to "get in there and fight" or quit. He said: "You men are beautifully endowed with talent, character, and family, and you can lead or you can follow. Even if no one else is, I am your friend, and you can come to me for help and counsel. But you must put out and give it your best, and if you do, Bowdoin will accept and honor you."

Bill Dean went on to hang up a great academic record at Bowdoin. For four years, Dean had nothing but straight A's in every course and kept this record up through his M.A. and Ph.D. at Harvard. He was a mental giant. However, tragedy followed. The Longfellow Prize is given to the junior who, up to that point, has achieved the best academic record. Although many thought Dean had earned it, the committee awarded the prize to another student. This broke Bill's heart. He brooded and lost weight and interest in life. He wouldn't go to class and locked himself in his study for days. He started to talk about suicide, and I literally sat on him for days, until he promised not to jump into the Androscoggin River.

The sequel to this is equally tragic. Bill graduated cum laude, Phi Beta Kappa, with honors in his major. He went on to Harvard and took his doctorate in economics. He maintained the same record there. He fully expected to be called back to his alma mater to teach, but the call never came. Twenty years later, brokenhearted over the failure of a U.N. mission to Tunisia which he headed, Bill returned to the United States. Ralph Bunche told Bill that no man could have succeeded in the harsh, unrealistic requirements of that U.N. mission. This was cold comfort to Dean. Failure overwhelmed him and early one blue morning he committed suicide. The world lost a brilliant, irreplaceable human being.

In 1970 at the 40th reunion of our class, Bowdoin honored me with the LL.D. degree. I am both proud and humble to have been singled out of my class to receive my alma mater's highest award. But the fact is overshadowed by the sorrow that Dean was not so rewarded. At our class retreat the night before the commencement of 1970, the class asked me to talk about my life and its storybook quality, but I could not. I felt compelled to tweak their consciences about the time in our junior year when Bill Dean was not given the Longfellow Prize. These classmates knew that Bill was a very brilliant man, not only in our class but also in the college, and more recognition should have been given him even after graduation. I asked why none of them had protested, why none went to bat for him, why none of them came to our room to offer consolation and fellowship.

Did this denial of just recognition lead to a lifetime of mental anguish that dictated the tragic and irretrievable suicide twenty years later? And if this tragic ending to a gifted life was not enough sorrow and heartbreak for one family, Bill's only son, unable to recover from the loss of his father, committed suicide a few years later. Sic transit gloria mundi!

Chapter Four

The Class of 1930 found itself job-hunting in the midst of the greatest depression this country has ever known. One suffered the helplessness of being caught in an earthquake. To those who did not go through it, words from one who did cannot adequately depict the despair, horror, and humiliation that overwhelmed Americans. As businesses collapsed and closed there were no jobs, especially for Blacks who were always on the periphery of employment. There was no money, no food, and no hope, except what was eventually supplied by a muddled and frantic government.

Etched deeply in my soul are vignettes from that period. I remember adult men and women searching garbage pails and street trash cans for scraps of food. Old men and young men stood in the bitter cold on the streets of our cities selling apples. Hungry, crying children and homeless men and women lurked in the shadows of office buildings and tenements. Temporary shacks were set up in vacant fields and parks. Starving humans, barefooted, ragged children, inched in long lines toward the soup kitchens of the Red Cross and the Salvation Army. I shall never forget the gaunt, haunted faces of bewildered people trying to hold on and survive.

My father had the impossible task of trying to reassure his flock that God had not forgotten them nor deserted them. Ministers and doctors are never paid in such a crisis, and father, with his own woes and troubles, had to administer to the afflictions of his numb and desolate parishioners while trying to keep his family alive and hopeful. But, miracle of miracles, our family never suffered from cold or hunger. We muddled through, and the common experience made us a stronger and more closely-knit band. We shared and shared alike, and each learned to feel a deep and sacred responsibility for all the others.

My sister Nellie, who was teaching by this time, helped to take up the slack in the family's paltry income. The teachers were paid with *script* and it could only be used locally and at those stores that would accept it. This script was a mere promise to pay when and if times got better. A few courageous storekeepers honored it and this enabled us to purchase basic food supplies.

The clarion voice of President Franklin D. Roosevelt finally rang through the murk of despair and chaos, and his confident demeanor and leadership brought hope and muscle back to a flabby and bewildered nation. His Works Progress Administration, Youth Conservation Corps, and National Recovery Programs produced temporary jobs and income. These new agencies, for the first time in history, gave Blacks an opportunity to hold white-collar jobs.

By the same token, these depression-made, stopgap policies produced the welfare or "relief" check for food and housing which was the beginning of an economic and psychological curse that has bedeviled Blacks ever since. Blacks since the dawn of slavery have been special pawns in the economic system of this country. They are the last hired on the upswing of the economy and the first fired when the economy sags. In a depression, jobs dry up and "relief" becomes the substitute for gainful employment. For many thousands who were unemployed or unemployable in the post-Depression market, "relief" became a way of life and has continued to be a way of life since the Thirties.

A Works Progress Administration program was set up in the Settlement House in Englewood, and my formal job history began when I was hired as a group worker under this program. I worked with teen-agers, supervising recreation programs. This was an effort to ease the strain of cold, foodless homes and counteract the despair that surrounded them there.

The staff at the Social Service Federation in Englewood was interracial, a radical departure for those days. Even in a depression the racial lines of this rich town were tightly drawn. The white staff members worked with the whites and the Black staff members worked with the Blacks. The staff was interracial because the social system at work in Englewood and generally in New Jersey dictated that whites teach or supervise whites, and Blacks teach or supervise Blacks in areas and institutions where there were social implications. There were separate days and hours for each group, and they seldom participated in integrated programs. The Fourth Ward, the area primarily served by the programs, was mostly composed of Blacks and Italians, and even though all of them were poor and deprived people, neither group wanted the onus of socializing with the other.

The salvation of the whole effort was the character and stature of the staff. The career staff was composed of professional social workers and they had been trained to care for the ills and problems of people. Crime, poverty, illness, and destitution were not particularly or peculiarly Black or white afflictions and the staff labored diligently to develop harmony among the groups that came to the Federation. I wish I could say as much for all of the volunteers. It was in this job that I learned my first adult lessons in the vagaries of race relations. The volunteer workers were Junior League girls from the wealthy hill families. Admission into the league required some form of public service, so they served, although not necessarily from conviction. They gave a few hours one day a week which taxed neither their mental nor physical strength. The leaguers were elegantly groomed and dressed, and when they left at five o'clock in chauffeured limousines, not a hair was out of place or a blouse or skirt wrinkled.

The volunteers read to the children, taught them parlor games, and supervised groups on sight-seeing trips. But few of these pampered, superficial girls probed the intricacies of the barren lives of the children in their care, and their pretended tolerance did little to sweeten their indifference. There was an almost unanimous failure to understand that being poor did not rob people of their right to dignity and pride. The condescending approach repelled and angered the recipients of their charity, and what the leaguers interpreted as "surliness" and "ingratitude" was a natural self-defense against that condescension.

What the rich thought of the benighted people in the Fourth Ward was indelibly shown at Christmastime. Big cars would glide down to the Social Service Federation laden with broken toys and unusable clothing: headless dolls, trackless trains, one-wheel bicycles, moth-eaten dresses, fingerless gloves, worn-out shoes, books on technical subjects, or sleds without runners. Even the eager desires of the hapless poor could not fix these useless things.

For me this stint at the Federation was a fascinating and productive period. I studied and probed the mannerisms and viewpoints, background and education of the volunteers and of the parents I met. Every facet of their being, from clothes to speech, reflected a similarity, and the WASP became for me alive and real. I got to know some of these girls and their parents very well. Our curiosities were mutual. As they tried to fathom my "difference," I plumbed their minds and motives.

In this way another job offer materialized. The father of one of the volunteers, Barbara Simpson, was vice chairman of the board of a Wall Street bank. Barbara felt I had too much ability to spend my life working in the Settlement House, and she asked her father to see if he could find a job for me in his bank. The doting father, ever anxious to indulge his only child, invited me to come to their sumptuous home for an interview. Barbara had a childish curiosity about what made people the way they were, and she admitted that my lack of self-consciousness of being a Black when in the presence of the wealthy hill whites, intrigued her. I arrived at 8:00 P.M. as requested, and was ushered into the paneled study by a liveried butler. Colonel Simpson soon entered the room, elegant in blue smoking jacket and red leather slippers. Sipping a brandy, he eyed me from head to foot before speaking, and then asked me what I had in mind. I knew there was no consequential job available to a Black in a Wall Street bank, so I pursued a tack that would make the colonel initiate suggestions of what he had had in mind when he asked me to come see him. I remained silent.

He was frank. He said that he never denied Barbara anything within his power to give and she had asked him to give me a job. He said his daughter was fascinated by my life and thought I should have a better opportunity to utilize my training. That was fine, he said in a brittle way, but where, and why, should he be the catalyst? He said there could hardly be a future in banking for Blacks, even if given the slightest chance to get into a bank or given the lowliest job. Well, perhaps a temporary something could be contrived to fit my case. He would talk with the employment officer at the bank and see if he could devise a slot for me.

I was to report to the colonel at 9:00 A.M. sharp in his office at One Wall Street the following Monday. The colonel then pushed the buzzer to summon the butler and told him to ask Barbara to come in. Barbara arrived with her mother in tow and introduced me. Colonel Simpson explained what he had decreed, and Barbara kissed him and congratulated me.

Colonel Simpson had every right to be puzzled about what to do about me. Since slavery, the Black had not been considered available for white-collar jobs. His alleged forte was as a domestic, farm worker, roustabout on wharves, or general laborer. The Depression gave Blacks en masse, the first white-collar opportunity in history. Before this, to have sought any kind of job short of janitorial in the corporate sector of America was risking insult and abuse. Monday morning I had a dickens of a time trying to convince the bank guards that I had an appointment with Colonel Simpson. He had forgotten to inform anyone and Blacks were just never seen in that bank.

Finally, one guard kept me under surveillance and another went to check out my story. Soon a red-faced flunky arrived to escort me to the colonel's office. I was introduced to a personnel officer who led me to less celestial quarters to brief me on my job.

I became a member of the bank messenger group, whose duties were the delivering of stocks and bonds to banks, financial houses, and the great corporations housed in the financial district. We often carried millions of dollars of negotiable bonds and stocks in little leather pouches strapped to our arms. These securities represented transactions completed in the stock market or some large financial deal. They had to be delivered promptly and placed in the hands of the right person. This corps of messengers was made up mostly of young men in their early twenties who were starting at the bottom in banking. A few were scions of great American families and they would eventually become stalwarts in the financial world. They had recently graduated from Ivy League schools and were serving short apprenticeships in this lowly station. They arrived in the morning with their squash racquets under their arms or with packed bags for a weekend of golf or tennis in the country. They were often called for in the evening by chauffeured cars, or rushed off by taxi to catch the 5:30 train to Westchester estates. For them my presence was a mystery. They were cool, curt, and snobbish and talked to me as little as possible.

I enjoyed the rush and bustle of Wall Street, and the heady atmosphere generated by the fabled Rockefellers and Morgans. Even during the Depression, the struggle for wealth went on with incessant fury, while stories of failures, suicides, and despondency filled every edition of the daily press. I tried to make myself believe this was a worthwhile job and experience, marking time until the "real thing" came along. It gave me insight into another world and another culture, and let me see behind the facade of wealth and power and caste. But every day as I rushed about the streets of lower New York, I had an uncomfortable premonition of impending failure, of being doomed to mediocrity and insignificance for a lifetime. After about six months my fellow employees helped to resolve my quandary, and I decided to try to find greener pastures.

One day in the "cage" where the securities were kept, my pouch had been filled with about $200,000 of negotiable bonds to be delivered immediately to a nearby bank. As usual I placed the pouch on my desk and went to the cloakroom for my coat and hat. When I returned, the pouch was missing. Consternation prevailed because the transaction had to be completed within the next thirty minutes or it would be void. While everyone in the office looked frantically for the pouch, the manager chastised me verbally for stupidity, incompetence, and perhaps criminality. I was devastated and frightened. I had left the pouch on my desk, as everyone did, to go to the cloakroom, and it was inconceivable that in a couple of minutes an outsider could have been admitted through guarded doors to snatch the pouch. A half hour later the pouch was found with contents intact, across the room under a stack of discarded financial journals. It must have been put there by one, or some, of my associates in order to have me miss the deadline of delivery and thereby lose my job. It had been thirty minutes of torture and nerve-wracking hell. I understood the not-so-subtle message.

Chapter Five

One of my few post-college social outlets was attendance at the monthly meetings of a graduate chapter of Alpha Phi Alpha fraternity. Alpha was the most prominent and oldest Black Greek letter college fraternity, and its prestige and social recognition in our community was high. The Alpha Alpha Mu graduate chapter of New Jersey contained the names of the most respected doctors, lawyers and teachers in the metropolitan area. At this time I was the youngest member and the chore of recording the minutes was foisted upon me. I tried to make the minutes interesting and humorous.

Lester B. Granger, Executive Secretary of the National Urban League, asked me one night after hearing me read the minutes if I'd like to work with *Opportunity* magazine, the official organ of the Urban League. He thought I could become an assistant to Elmer Carter, the editor, and perhaps eventually the business manager. Since the League was struggling just to stay alive, the salary would be small but the opportunity and experience would be great. I accepted, and this permitted me to resign from my messenger job at the bank with legitimacy and honor.

In those days the Urban League and the National Association for the Advancement of Colored People were the only two national organizations fighting to redress the social and economic ills that afflicted American Blacks. The League concentrated on housing and jobs, while the militant NAACP fought for civil rights and human decency. Because they had the pick of the Black college men and women who did not want to teach and could not find other avenues open for upward mobility, these two organizations had staffs of eminent people. Although the Depression was over, for Blacks there was still no choice of career. Only segregated avenues of life were open and they usually meant domestic or menial jobs or, if one was very lucky, the post office or pullman porter service. Naturally, I rejoiced at the chance to work with an acknowledged giant of the Black world and to be a part of the continuing crusade against discrimination and caste.

What a break for me at this period of an uncharted career to be thrown into association with Elmer Anderson Carter! A Harvard graduate and former Urban League secretary in Louisville, he was a brilliant wordsmith and a writer of exceptional clarity and style. His editorials were gems and his speeches rang with an authority that held his audiences spellbound. Elmer was a raconteur, a bon vivant, a connoisseur of good food and drink, a comedian, and a kind and gracious man. To share a meal with him was a rich experience, and to be his audience was a treat sought after by all who knew him. His one vice was his hatred of work and he shunned difficult tasks with skill. Meeting press deadlines was particularly offensive to him, so he welcomed my staff debut with elation. I soaked up his passion for excellence in the spoken and written word and copied some of his mannerisms for telling anecdotes and making speeches. He encouraged me to use pen and tongue to help break the bonds of inequality that kept our race in social and economic subjection.

I worked for the National Urban League for two years, and

moved on to the NAACP in order to get deeper into the fight against the twin evils of segregation and discrimination. The NAACP was locked in a struggle with Congress to obtain legislation outlawing lynching and peonage, and the call to Black America for financial support and personal involvement touched my soul deeply.

I joined the NAACP in 1937 at one of the great moments in American political and social history. It was the beginning of President Roosevelt's second term, and he was still trying to stabilize the economy after the ravages of the Great Depression. It was the era when the NAACP was trying to appeal to the conscience of America to pass legislation to stop the rash of brutal lynchings. It also was unveiling the not-so-hidden system of peonage on the great farms of the South.

James Weldon Johnson as executive secretary and W.E.B. DuBois as editor of *Crisis* magazine, the official organ of the NAACP, had developed the NAACP into the strongest and most effective Black protest organization in our country's history. At the time I joined, Dr. DuBois had just resigned and Johnson had been succeeded by Walter White. As a boy I had read of the exploits of James Weldon Johnson and Dr. DuBois and Dean William Pickens as they carried the message of the organization throughout the country. Pickens was field secretary and he had faced mobs in the South and fearlessly proclaimed the right of Black folks, even in lynching territory. I wanted to be a part of this crusade and I, too, was ready to lay my life on the line to carry the message to beleaguered Blacks in the dark recesses of the nation.

The national staff was a small one. Roy Wilkins, an astute, able young man from Minnesota, was the assistant secretary and editor of *The Crisis*. Thurgood Marshall was just beginning his assault upon the discriminatory teachers' salary structure of the South, and maturing for future legal greatness under the tutelage of Charles Houston, general counsel of the NAACP. Also on the board were William Hastie, Dean of Howard Law School; and Arthur Spingarn, famous lawyer; brilliant, youthful Juanita Jackson of Baltimore, youth secretary; and George Murphy, Jr., also of Baltimore, press officer. Our pay was minimal and often zero. It depended upon the success of membership drives in the branches. In the early post-Depression years we had many payless paydays. This meant that all the staff members were dedicated people who stayed because of a conviction that they were fortunate participants in the cause of Black freedom and equality.

At that time the Association had about six hundred branches throughout the country. I was to work under the supervision of Dean Pickens as "Coordinator of Branches." Pickens was a dynamic speaker and, especially in the South, his name was gold. He had been Dean at Talladega College in Alabama, and his former students were potential branch members and leaders wherever they resided.

Dean Pickens took me by the hand and taught me how to "survive" in the Deep South. The youthful spirit of an educated, self-sufficient, fluent northerner had to be tempered to fit the suspicious, dangerous, uncompromising attitude of the white South. The Dean nurtured my sense of humor so it would become a valuable part of my arsenal for survival in the scores of little towns, north and south, where intolerance and bigotry were woven into the fabric of community life. My task was to coordinate activity and develop programs of a uniform nature that would increase membership and add to the flow of funds to the national office. It meant developing leadership and programs that fitted each branch and giving local members hope and determination and courage. It took a lot of the latter to espouse the cause of Blacks in the Deep South, or the border states, or even in the Middle West.

If my success were to be measured by the money raised on my branch visits or funding campaigns, it could only be rated fair. However, I would get a higher rating for the Christmas Seal program which was put under my direction. But the growth in my awareness of the plight of Black people in America and my conviction that my life must be dedicated to their cause rates highest marks.

I remember an incident which occurred in Baton Rouge, Louisiana, in 1938. It left a scar on my soul. The Baton Rouge branch had been intimidated and harassed by the Ku Klux Klan. The youthful branch president, Leon Wallace, an insurance executive, decided that this was the time for the branch to be active rather than quiescent. He asked me to come to speak at a rally to be held in one of the large churches. Wallace had been warned by the mayor, the chief of police, and the head of the local Klan to cancel the meeting. Then the pastor of the church where the meeting was to be held was threatened and told that his church would be burned.

I arrived in town on the day of the rally. The tension was awful. The Black professionals had refused to attend the meeting. They locked themselves inside their homes that night. Then the pastor of the church backed off and we were left without a meeting place. However, a courageous minister from a smaller church took up the challenge and said we could meet there. We accepted.

Leon Wallace and his friend, Horatio Thompson, a young filling-station owner, exhibited that night the kind of courage one seldom finds. They issued a public statement that the meeting would be held even if we had to assemble on the banks of the Mississippi and that Morrow would speak. Despite the mayor, the Klan, and the timidity of the Black professionals, Leon Wallace, Horatio Thompson, Reverend Jones and I walked with scores of townspeople that night: artisans, blue collar workers, domestics, poolroom habitués, skid row denizens, to the banks of the Mississippi River and then to the church to hold our meeting. It was the most gutsy, inspiring and emotional gathering I've ever spoken to, and that night I made a vow never, never to shrink from fear, never to lack courage to walk the hard road to freedom.

On another occasion I went to Indianapolis to revive an all-but-dead branch. The two weeks I was there were tough sledding because the branch had not fulfilled its mission and this town, the former stronghold and home of the Ku Klux Klan, had killed all initiative in the few remaining members. Robert De Frantz, secretary of the local YMCA, was a strong member of the Black community. He had great influence and wide contacts and was instrumental in keeping alive in the city on an interracial basis some cultural and civic activities. Once a year the YMCA sponsored a citywide program in a cultural series on Black history and achievement. The speaker was always a prominent, nationally-known figure. Dr. DuBois and

James Weldon Johnson had been speakers in the past and this was an eagerly anticipated event in Indianapolis and the house was always full. This year Walter White was the guest speaker.

I stayed at the YMCA and came to know De Frantz well. He accompanied me to two or three neighborhood meetings as I tried to encourage rebuilding of the branch and he was moved by my passionate appeal to civic responsibility and challenge to duty. To my surprise, nevertheless, De Frantz asked me to sit on the platform the night of the YMCA program and to my further surprise he introduced me and asked me to speak to the audience for five minutes. My impromptu speech contained the message I had been taking around the country for two years and it was rewarded by an audience that stood and applauded for five minutes when I sat down.

In July 1942, at the national convention of the NAACP in Los Angeles, I was asked to make a short speech in behalf of the youth of the organization. As the theme I took the title "Morituri Salutamus" ("We who are about to die salute you") of the famous poem written by Henry Wadsworth Longfellow, Bowdoin's great alumnus, for the 50th reunion of his class of 1825. I knew I would soon be inducted into the Army, as would many other young men who were there. The theme carried the hopes of youth drafted for war. Many of them would never return.

Now, forty years later, it is easy to forget what conditions were like for Blacks in those days.

Chapter Six

Sunday, December 7, 1941, was a beautiful day. I was happy to be taking the scenic ferry boat ride from the Battery at the foot of Wall Street to Staten Island. There I was to address the Staten Island chapter of the NAACP at 1:00 P.M. I arrived at the church where the meeting was to be held at 12:30, and already a few people were in the pews. At 12:55 as I was mounting the rostrum with the president of the branch, the church door was flung open and an excited man dashed down the aisle yelling, "The Japanese have just bombed Pearl Harbor, and President Roosevelt has declared war!" The church emptied as if someone had yelled "Fire!" and I found myself standing alone in the pulpit. As I hurried back to the pier to catch the next boat to Manhattan, radios were blaring and people were shouting and rushing about the streets in a frenzy. It hit me like a slap that this was the end of an era and the beginning of a frightening, unknowable future.

The attack on Pearl Harbor made the draft a reality for most able-bodied men between 19 and 35. I was 31 years old at the time, and, for the time being, safe from the draft call. However, I was single and, as an NAACP staff member, probably not in a civilian occupation considered vitally necessary to the success of U.S. war efforts. A few weeks after the first nationwide draft call, the draft number of my younger brother, William, a sophomore at Rutgers University, was picked, and he was hustled off forthwith to a training camp in the South.

In July, 1942, the draft board notified me to appear before them. Immediately upon my return from the national convention of the NAACP in Los Angeles, I went before them to be told to hold myself ready for induction in the fall. This was still the day of the segregated army and navy, and draft boards received quotas for Blacks and whites to meet the needs determined by the Pentagon.

Segregated units of Black soldiers in the army had been a tradition of the United States since the Revolutionary War. In that war some patriots were afraid to arm Black slaves, thinking the British might outstrip them in arming both Blacks and Indians. However, individual Blacks distinguished themselves in the war. Lemuel Haynes served as a Minuteman, and Peter Salem at Bunker Hill killed Major Pitcairn, leader of the British forces. Pompey, a Black, worked out the plan for the capture of Stony Point by Mad Anthony Wayne in 1779, and 5000 Blacks were on guard at General Washington's camp when Cornwallis surrendered at Yorktown in 1781. Lincoln authorized the raising of Negro troops after the Proclamation of Emancipation. Before the end of the war they aggregated 178,975—commanded altogether by white officers. These troops were not treated as equal to white troops, and they did not receive the same compensation.

In World War I the system continued. Blacks had to register under methods of discrimination, that they might not be confused with whites. In the beginning no provisions were made for training Black officers, and certain congressmen urged that all Blacks be confined to stevedore regiments. They were commanded mainly by illiterate, prejudiced white men, who subjected them to incomparable hardships.

Since my induction was inevitable, I decided to "volunteer" and take advantage of the Pentagon's announcement that volunteers with the right physical and educational qualifications could take thirteen weeks of basic training and then go directly to Officer's Candidate School. I notified my draft board in August that I proposed to take advantage of this option and I was assigned to a contingent leaving the Bergen County Court House in Hackensack on the morning of August 21st for Fort Dix, New Jersey. In this group were 31 men. I was the only Black. They had all volunteered for OCS. These men had been policemen, artisans, bookkeepers, clerks and plumbers' helpers. At best they had been to high school. I was the only college man in the group. At dawn with a former police sergeant in charge, we boarded a bus for the trip to Fort Dix. I left behind a tearfully sad mother and sister, and found a place for myself in the rear of the bus where I could reflect and compose myself for whatever lay ahead.

We arrived at Dix a little before noon and our rigid physical examination began at once. I was 6′1″ and weighed 135 pounds, facts which had made me the butt of jokes for a long time. But the doctors found my skinny frame durable and tough and virile. After the physical, those of us who passed were led off to another building to take examinations to determine if we had the minimum intelligence necessary to qualify us for OCS. I found the test extremely simple and finished it in forty minutes instead of the ninety minutes allotted for it. It was of grammar school level and I wondered why OCS candidates were given such simple fare.

At the close of the examination I sat outside the barracks where the session had been held until a major emerged with a list in his hand and called my name. He asked me to come with him and we reentered the building. Closing the door, he told me to sit down. He had a funereal look on his face which puzzled me, but which became clear as soon as he spoke. "Mr. Morrow," he purred, "you failed the written examination. We are sorry, because you looked like good material, but that's the way it is. Take this paper and report back to your draft board for further instructions."

I was too stunned to ask any questions and stumbled out of

the room to find the return bus home. No one else failed. The ride home was torture. I was bursting with anger and consumed by frustration. I hadn't failed that test! If anything, I probably answered 99 percent of the questions correctly. There was no way I could have failed.

Before we arrived in Hackensack I finally came to grips with myself and in my own mind solved the riddle. Shortly before I left my job at the NAACP I remembered how there had been a struggle to try to get the military authorities to develop a definite policy for Black officers. It was refused. I remembered that the decision had been made to have as few Black officers as possible in the armed forces, and certainly not to recruit any. I remembered that most of the Black units already on active duty had white officers, and that the door was effectively slammed in the faces of any new aspirants. Truly, this blue day at Fort Dix was a signal of my future life in the army.

At 7:00 A.M. on Monday, November 4, 1942, I again boarded a bus, this time with forty-five other draftees, and left the Court House for Fort Dix. It was the real thing this time. Those of us aboard the bus had passed our physicals and been declared good, sound material. I was one of the oldest draftees aboard. Most of the men were in their early twenties and seemed carefree as we sped toward the camp. Two of the ten blacks aboard were from Hackensack, Russell Everett and Victor Bland. Our families had known each other for many years. They were the age of my younger brother William. William had finished his training at OCS and was already aboard a transport bound for North Africa. These young men clung to me because of my maturity and appearance of having a "stiff upper lip," but our conversation all the way to Dix was full of misgivings and trepidation.

Upon arrival at the camp we were steered into a large building to take the I.Q. test. There did not appear to be any future career riding on the score I made, but I took pains to do well. Only some months later would I learn the results. The group of draftees on our bus was composed of Blacks and whites, but after the I.Q. exam was finished, when barrack assignments were made, the old Jim Crow pattern of segregation took over.

My barracks was a big tent with five other men assigned to it. It was pitched on the hard surface of the parade ground beside a row of clapboard barracks. The tent was open at the top near the ridgepole and the sides were very porous. Inside, six army cots stood about a foot off the ground. The dark, cold interior was a depressing sight to a recruit who just six hours before had climbed out of his own warm, comfortable bed at home. All my life I have been susceptible to colds and would never go out-of-doors in the winter without scarf and hat, to say nothing about sleeping in unheated quarters. However, here I was, under new auspices, and I would sleep anywhere the army placed me and wear whatever clothing was provided for the occasion. My tentmates were a motley crew. They were all in their twenties and from varying backgrounds, obviously deprived ones. Their horizons had always been low and each of them bore marks of America's racial caste system. Our conversation was commonplace and primarily concerned with guessing where we would be shipped and the latest rumors.

Fort Dix was essentially a collection area for recruits as well as a debarkation point for trained troops leaving for overseas. Recruits were kept at Dix for a few days' orientation and classification. After this most would be shipped out to other stations for training and future assignment. I was at Fort Dix at least two weeks beyond the normal period. The problem was one of classification. The first effort to classify me ended in a fiasco. The not-too-bright sergeant in charge of this service went strictly by the large book he consulted. It supposedly contained every possible classification of human endeavor. My record card indicated that I had been coordinator of branches of the NAACP. The sergeant therefore spent one-half hour trying to find the classification "coordinator." Then he said to me: "Hey, private, there ain't no classification for you. I can't assign you to any unit until headquarters has a look. We'll keep you in a pool here until further notice." The idea of "classification" was, of course, to try to place recruits where their civilian skills could be put to use. However, many times it did not work out because of confusion and ineptness at induction centers. Shoemakers ended up in the medics, carpenters as bakers, and plumbers with the military police.

At 1:00 A.M. one chilly morning, along with 499 other recruits, I was routed out of bed and marched about a mile to the camp rail yard where, under the cover of darkness and very secret orders, we boarded rickety passenger cars for a faraway ride to an "unknown" destination. We were crowded into the old, cold, dirty cars like cattle and, since all window shades were drawn, we had no idea of where we were or where we were going. After twenty-four hours of these miserable conditions, we pulled into a drab, desolate place and unloaded. Now we were told where we were: Camp Sutton, three miles from Monroe, North Carolina. God certainly ignored this place in creating the earth. It was a miserable wasteland of red clay and forests, and man and machines were trying to develop the elementary creature comforts to house and train thousands of soldiers of war.

We were Black, so we were marched three miles at 2:00 A.M. (instead of being trucked) to an undeveloped section. We would live in tents until we could fashion something better with our hands. This was a brutal, cruel introduction to Jim Crow life in the army. Tired, hungry, and lame we dragged ourselves and our gear over a primitive trail through the mud and the woods. "Way out yonder" would be the place we'd get ready for our home while we learned the art of war, or rather, how to perform the support services for white troops.

Camp Sutton was a horrible experience. The five hundred men sent from Dix were to form a battalion euphemistically called "Quartermasters," but which was really a labor battalion. A labor battalion lifted freight, dug trenches and latrines, built roads, trucked supplies, erected tents and buildings—performed any tasks which involved manual labor.

The majority of the men were semi-literate. The officers were whites, right out of OCS with the rank of second lieutenant. Many of the recruits from the deep South had little, if any, schooling and had been picked up in bars or poolrooms by sheriffs and sent off to the Army to fill a quota set up by draft authorities for the state. I discovered scores of men who had been railroaded into the service, leaving behind them families who had no idea where they were.

There were about ten college-trained men in the battalion, and early in the development of the outfit we got together to lay plans for more humane treatment. After thirty days I was promoted to sergeant and immediately started using the little authority given me to inspire the men to develop self-respect, pride and courage.

For bathing there was one cold water hose per company. We had no indoor toilets or plumbing, no reading material, no chaplain, no place to congregate, and no recreational facilities of any sort. In the white areas the soldiers had movies, recreation halls and reading rooms, but we were barred from all these areas. After we finished training on those long, cold winter days, there was no place to go but back to our tents, blackened with the soot of the soft coal used in the small stoves. It was deadly, dull and demoralizing.

The nearby town of Monroe was a hell hole. It was the lair of prostitutes, gamblers, con men, venereal disease, lurid movies, and tourist traps. Funny thing: these were all off limits to Black soldiers and in town there was little available to them but trouble. The local police and white M.P.s used the Black soldiers for target practice and "dry runs" on police practice of simulated problems. Every payday, trucks and M.P. vans drove up to our area and dropped off bloody, beaten hulks of men who had run afoul of the lawmen in Monroe. The men could have been merely looking in shop windows or standing on a corner watching the passersby. But they were victims of white hate, thought to be possible rapists or "social equality" seekers, and they had to be "kept in their place." The incidence of venereal disease in our outfit was staggering, and special toilets were built in the woods for use by those afflicted. These circumstances were hard to take and added to the terror and inhumaneness of this camp. The men wanted me to be their spokesman on all occasions, even though I was powerless to challenge the inequities and injustices of our pitiful condition.

On Sunday mornings I assembled the men of Company 'A' and served as chaplain. I would preach from a text that illustrated courage and hope and bid them to hold on checking their fears and their anger. I told them that eventually we would overcome. However, lying distraught and despairing on my cot in the bitter cold darkness of the tent, I wondered how, under the present odds, we would overcome!

Two of the most able and intelligent men of the battalion were sergeants William Bryant and Harold Amos. Both were from southern New Jersey, college-trained, and occupying significant positions in the battalion. Amos was battalion sergeant-major and Bryant was in headquarters. They had access to the cables and correspondence passing through headquarters, and these could often shed light on the strange things going on in the camp. We became good friends and shared our off-duty time reading, walking and discussing the future of the battalion and our own futures. We had hopes of going to OCS, but the prospects were dim. However, we agreed we had to keep our eyes open and be prepared in every way for the possibility.

One day Bryant came to me with startling news. He had looked at our files in headquarters and noted that on the I.Q. test I had taken at the processing center in Dix the score read 105 but that someone had gone over the score with ink-eradicator and changed the middle number from five to zero. So I had made a score of 155 on that test after all! The 105 made it too low for OCS. The minimum score for OCS was 110. Waves of anger and frustration swept over me. If I were not to do irreparable damage to my nervous system and self-esteem, some method would have to be devised to get an airing for this situation. But how could an anonymous Black soldier combat the vicious system facing Black troops?

Our first sergeant, a Black, was a regular Army soldier who because of both educational and social limitations had learned to accept without question the segregated and discriminatory system of the military. He owed his rank and perquisites to a grinning, amiable demeanor in the presence of whites and disciplined his Black troops with an iron hand. He was deaf to pleas or petitions for recognition of human, civil, or constitutional rights. He carried out the decrees and enforced the mores of the southern social system and would not brook any effort of his men to speak to the commanding officer about grievances. Since we would have to go through the first sergeant to get to the commanding officer, a bold plan would have to be formulated to overcome this primary obstacle.

I asked the first sergeant for permission to see my personal file relative to my score on the I.Q. test taken at Fort Dix. The request was, of course, denied. I then asked permission to speak to the C.O. This too was denied. And, adding a gratuitous insult, the sergeant flayed me for being "a pompous, uppity, trouble-making Black." He told me to try to learn how to "soldier" and to stop trying to buck the system.

In desperation I wrote a letter to Mr. John Borg, editor and publisher of the Bergen Evening Record, the principal newspaper of my home county. Borg was a rich, powerful Republican, and he wielded great influence nationally, as well as locally. He had great respect for my father and his efforts to raise and educate a family in the anti-Black atmosphere of Hackensack. I hoped that an inquiry from him at the proper level might loosen the logjam. I could now only sit and wait.

Then one day I was summoned to headquarters to talk to a warrant officer in personnel. The summons was startling and unexpected. The officer showed me my I.Q. test folder from Fort Dix and pointed out to me the dismal mark of 105, five points shy of the minimum needed to apply for OCS. In anger I pointed to the attempted erasure of the five and the insertion of a zero in the score, and stood up to leave. The officer told me to sit down. He feigned ignorance of the occurrence and stammered a weak explanation. I told him his explanation was unsatisfactory and that I wanted to see the Battalion Commander. He said no. I stood up, saluted and walked out. Twenty-four hours later, the first sergeant told me to go to headquarters to take a new I.Q. test. I did. The score was 156.

What had happened? Mr. Borg took my problem directly to the Secretary of the Army, suggesting that such blatant discrimination could not bear public airing and should be corrected promptly or become a subject for congressional debate with attendant publicity.

Now I had passed the test again. I put in a request for an appearance before the OCS board. A week later I was called before the board and questioned at length. These grim-faced, solemn officers gave me no hint of their verdict. I must wait until notified "in due course." Whatever the consequences, I knew I had performed well and honestly, and I could live with myself for the rest of the war.

After we had been at Camp Sutton for six months we

learned that we were to participate in war maneuvers in Tennessee. They were already in progress and were distinguished by the emergence of a brilliant Brigadier General, Dwight D. Eisenhower. The tempo of our training increased and we were tired but hardened troops when we boarded shuttered rail coaches for the trip to Tullahoma.

We arrived in Tullahoma at five in the morning after a twenty-four hour trip and were immediately trucked to a marshy area near a river to pitch our tents. We tried to gather enough hay from nearby fields to cover the damp ground beneath our tents. Not only was the area damp and forbidding but it was part of a dense forest, and as night fell it became eerie and black and ominous. The officers did not set up tents. Instead they were billeted in the trucks. The troops also gathered hay to line the body of the trucks so the officers could spread their bedrolls there.

About 2:00 A.M. that night, the camp was startled by loud screams. Pandemonium broke out, and men ran scrambling through the woods in panic. Flashlight beams shone in a hundred directions as the soldiers tried to find out what was going on. Officers were shouting commands, and bewildered guards were yelling "Halt!" as dim figures ran through their positions. When the confusion subsided, the cause of the uproar was discovered. In that area there is a kind of snake that suns itself all day in the branches of tall trees. When night comes and the temperature drops, the snakes uncoil and drop to the ground. Some fell on the tents and others landed on the ground and crawled into the tents to find warmth. When they crawled into the cots with the men, all hell broke loose! Some of the men were badly bitten and others so paralyzed with fright that they needed medication to calm their hysteria. The officers, annoyed that their sleep had been interrupted, told the troops to be "men" and return to their tents and settle down. Then the officers climbed back into the trucks and went back to sleep. Either the command had to find a new camp site or face a demoralized battalion. In any event, after this episode I knew I did not want to go overseas with this command and hoped for some miracle of transfer. It happened!

We were on the rifle range one cold, damp day when a

messenger from headquarters came out to "jeep" me in to see the base adjutant. The adjutant handed me a sheaf of papers, and these turned out to be processing papers and orders sending me to the Officer's Candidate School at Fort Lee, Virginia. I have never known a happier day. This call to go to OCS rescued me from the swamps and snakes of Tennessee and gave me a chance to work for military justice for Blacks from an improved vantage point. My comrades cheered to see one of their group break out of the swamp of despair and head for higher ground. Perhaps other Blacks would follow.

Chapter Seven

Officer's Candidate School offered an interesting variation on the prejudice I'd experienced so far in the service. My entering class was #48, and there were about ten Blacks in a class of 200. There was one other Black in my company. We were housed with our white mates but the social areas were off limits to us just as they had been at Camp Sutton and on maneuvers.

I did well at OCS because I liked challenge and rugged competition. It was the first time that I had been exposed to the necessity of conquering the rigors of a very physical existence in competition with hundreds of other men and it was truly the survival of the fittest and the brightest. Many of the candidates failed and after each test it was gratifying to stand at roll call and receive your "pass" grade from an officer. The best officer candidate was selected to command the graduating battalion on graduation day. I was chosen. However, forty-eight hours before the ceremony I was blandly told by an officer that since the governor of Virginia and other high officials would be present, it might be an affront to them to have a Black commanding the 250 graduating second lieutenants.

My sister, Nellie, came down for graduation to pin on my officer bars. After the ceremony none of the white taxi drivers would give us a lift out of camp. This was my first insult as a U.S. Army officer. It hurt more than being deprived of the rank of cadet commander at graduation.

After a fifteen-day leave, I returned to Fort Lee to await assignment. It was another devastating experience. There were over fifty officers, left over from previous classes, in the "Black pool." No assignments for them had been made. It was a cute way to handle the situation. By admitting a few Blacks to the OCS classes in the various services of the Army (i.e., Quartermasters, Infantry, Engineers, and so on) the national Black community's cry of discrimination was quieted. However, the Army had no intention of using them in combat commands. Thus, scores of Black officers piled up in "pools" at various points awaiting assignment.

At Camp Lee we were in a segregated barracks, ate in a segregated mess hall, and were denied admission to the officers' club or other recreational facilities in the complex. We could do nothing but wait. It was tedious, boring, and frustrating. An attempt was made to schedule classes for us in "automobile maintenance," for example. Many of the officers remained in the pool so long that they repeated the series of classes two and three times. In the large mess hall white officers in the pool ate in a well-furnished dining room on one side of a partition. The Black side of the partition, by contrast, was poorly appointed and a lieutenant colonel sat at the head of a table for six with the back legs of his chair in the kitchen door. Our white counterparts laughed outright at us and made loud and insulting jokes on their side of the partition. The situation of the Black pool was a disgrace to the Army, the country, and a dastardly insult to the men who were its victims.

After a month of this, I revolted. I called a meeting and eighteen of our thirty officers attended. We decided to send a petition to the commanding general of Fort Lee, asking him to redress our grievances and permit us to receive the dignity and courtesies to which our rank and uniform and citizenship entitled us. Ten men signed the petition and I hand-delivered it to the general's office. The response was fast and effective! I was reprimanded for attempting to lead a mutiny and ordered forthwith to Camp Shanks, New York, for immediate shipment overseas. The other nine who signed were counseled about their imprudence and were put on standby for shipment elsewhere in the near future.

Camp Shanks was a sprawling installation carved out of the wooded area of Orange County. It was about thirty miles from the debarkation docks in Hoboken, New Jersey. Interestingly enough, the camp was only twenty-five miles from my hometown but leave restrictions were so severe in debarkation areas it might as well have been five hundred miles away. I reported to a quartermaster trucking battalion about to depart for Europe. Its officers were mostly white, and the half-dozen Black officers were all new second lieutenants with neither enough rank nor command authority to be effective. After reporting late that afternoon there was nothing to do but find my barracks and wait until the next morning to be assigned to duties.

With two other recently arrived Black officers I sallied forth to the officers' club for a drink. But the "color line" was alive and well in New York State, too. When we opened the door, a white sergeant seated behind a desk greeted us with "Where the hell do you niggers think you're going? This is a white officers' club." That crude remark ignited our anger, and within five minutes the club was a shambles. The white military police responded to the alarm and, after we were pummeled and shoved and further insulted, we were placed under arrest. At the hearing the next day, the colonel commanding the battalion said: "This lieutenant came to my outfit as a militant troublemaker. He sowed seeds of discontent at Fort Lee and tried to get the other Black officers there to precipitate a state of anarchy. I want no part of him, for he will probably have my troops in a state of rebellion before we get past the Statue of Liberty."

Twenty-four hours later I was handed orders to report at

once to the office of the special assistant to the Secretary of the Army at the Pentagon in Washington. There a Black official in the Secretary's office gave me a dressing down that was classic. Among other things he said: "Morrow, this is your last chance. You are no longer in the NAACP but the United States Army, so stop your damn crusading for civil rights and soldier! One more offense and you'll be on your way to Leavenworth!"

I left the Pentagon with orders to report to the Information and Education School for Officers at Washington and Lee University in Lexington, Virginia. This was an advanced school to train officers to lecture to troops on all facets of war, and set up educational facilities to help bring backward troops up to the level of at least an eighth grade education. Putting an officer in this category took him out of the chain of command. However, it was a powerful weapon if you used it correctly. The course at Washington and Lee was for three to six months, but I was there for only six weeks. Lexington was sacred territory in the Old Confederacy. General Robert E. Lee became president of the college after the Civil War and his tomb on the campus is a shrine. Students from the adjacent Virginia Military campus salute Lee's tomb as they pass by. As I also crossed the campus daily, it was often difficult for the cadets to salute the tomb and then turn to salute me. Maybe this dilemma speeded up my departure from Washington and Lee.

Chapter Eight

My orders directed me to proceed forthwith from Washington and Lee to another embarkation camp in the Pennsylvania mountains: Indiantown Gap Military Reservation. It is located in a pass through a chain of mountains and is windy, cold and desolate. At any given time it held ten to twenty thousand troops in transit overseas. It was both a training ground and a departure point for Black stevedore troops, euphemistically called "transportation companies." All officers of both camp personnel and troops were white. Otherwise the camp was rigidly segregated. When I arrived to become the head of information and education for all Black troops, there was one other Black second lieutenant in the camp.

Fortunately, Colonel Forrester Ambrose, commanding the Black section of the camp, was a decent, honorable and religious man. A career Army officer, Colonel Ambrose was the son of a Presbyterian minister. He believed in fair play and equal opportunity and spent twenty-four hours a day fighting to secure equal treatment and training for the Black troops at the Gap. He was hated by white officers and men alike because of his mission, and he was harried and sabotaged and finally destroyed by his own white staff officers. Their anger over his liberal policies for Black troops led to myriad complaints to higher headquarters for his removal. Colonel Ambrose liked and respected me. He felt that my spirit and courage were qualities that all Black troops had to develop to win in battle, both in and out of the Army. He supported me at every step and, as a result, we were both targeted for oblivion and destruction. This could be achieved by bad efficiency reports from Inspection Teams from the Pentagon who would interview tattling officers with anti-Black feelings and attitudes.

Here again, these thousands of Black troops had no recreational facilities or outlet for leisure time. Just a mile away in the main part of the camp there were recreation halls, sport fields, guest houses, and hostesses for the white troops. Colonel Ambrose was determined to build these facilities for his Black troops, and while he succeeded in part, it contributed to his undoing. For example, Black troops, returning hot and tired from all-day training in the field, could hear the happy yells of white soldiers in their swimming pool a few hundred yards away. Colonel Ambrose juggled funds under his jurisdiction and started to build a swimming pool for his Black troops. But the commanding general halted the construction and reprimanded the colonel severely for extravagance and poor judgment.

In the winter months, the wind and snow whistled down from the mountains and buried the camp. In summer it was a baked desert. Training under these conditions was difficult and discouraging, but every week hundreds of men marched out of the camp late at night and boarded trains in Harrisburg en route to the battlegrounds of the world.

When I arrived at the Gap, I recognized the familiar state of low morale and the paranoia among the troops toward their unsympathetic white officers. I became the "chaplain," father confessor, counselor, and defender of the truth. It was a dangerous, vulnerable, "you're-asking-for-it" position.

I selected from the companies four college-bred sergeants for my staff. They were tough, able, intelligent and courageous. We forged a program of lectures on Black American history that fired the emotions and flung a challenge to the troops. The lectures engendered race spirit, a sense of personal worth, and a determination to do the best job of soldiering ever done anywhere. The course was so successful that it frightened the commanders. An investigation was called for and the Pentagon sent a team of white officers to the Gap to see what it was all about.

One afternoon I was ordered by the Chief of Training to give a "typical" lecture to about 250 troops. My subject was "We Were Always There." It told the history of the Black contribution to every U.S. war from the Revolutionary War to Pearl Harbor, and my illustrations were Crispus Attucks, the first American to die in the Revolutionary War; Peter Salem, the hero of Bunker Hill; General Washington's Negro Guard at Yorktown; the Black Boston regiment at Antietam; the old 15th New York regiment at Chateau Thierry; Dorie Miller at Pearl Harbor, and a host of others. And then I continued thusly:

> "and so today we need particularly to remember why these Negroes persevered until death . . . so that we could live in dignity and walk this world and this land in peace and self assurance. Despite our ancestors' deathless achievements, we are today in this and dozens of camps across the nation enveloped in thoughtful anxiety as we evaluate the current efforts here and abroad to destroy the moral, spiritual and intellectual effects of our accomplishments and contributions to our country over 100 years. This is hard to take. Why at this critical stage of our history of loyalty and development in our native land are we harassed and damned and pricked by a wave of oppression and insult that engulfs our very souls?
>
> We know that we have fought the good fight and kept the faith; we have been loyal in the face of odds that might have overcome weaker men; we have offered our lives on battlefields around the world for the preservation of a philosophy of life that did not include us; we fought then—and we'll fight now—because of a rugged faith that believes . . .
>
> 'This land is ours by right of birth,

This land is ours by right of toil,
We helped to till its virgin earth,
Our sweat is in its fruitful soil!'"

When I finished, the room exploded like a rocket. The men screamed and yelled and danced and ran up to the platform to mob me with thanks and praise. The delegation of officers who had come to judge sat stiff and silent and red-faced. They left without comment or greeting. The next day I was summoned to face a board of officers, who were to sit in judgment not only on my performance of the day before, but my fitness to continue at that post. It was all stated briefly by a lieutenant colonel who headed the board:

"Your lectures go beyond the bounds of military necessity. You incite troops. Those men yesterday left with a glint in their eyes and they are now ready to raise hell. If Washington decides to leave you here, you will tone down your talks and not use inflammatory material or tones. You will confine yourself to material sent to you by headquarters and not freewheel at the Army's expense. One member of the board from the Pentagon said your speech was 'almost Communistic.' You are therefore relieved of further lectures until your case is thoroughly reviewed."

Colonel Ambrose went straight to the War Department about this. He said that I made the difference between anarchy and a successful training program at the Gap, and the white officers commanding these departing units would be safer leaving the Gap with my lectures ringing in their troops' ears than with the hatred aroused by segregated training and mean treatment burning in their hearts and souls!

Colonel Ambrose was a Regular Army officer, who, although able and efficient, had been a victim of the archaic promotion system practiced before World War II. He had served as a captain for over twelve years and had risen rapidly since the declaration of war on December 7, 1941. He had served with Black troops before and was sympathetic toward them. He was also a practicing Christian and fought tirelessly to improve their condition. In the context of the war effort, these personal qualities of the colonel were in conflict with the aim and the mood of the U.S. war machine and he often came a cropper in his plans and efforts. Despite being hamstrung constantly, Colonel Ambrose did a splendid job of whipping Black troops into shape for service overseas. They responded to his efforts on their behalf and they knew how he risked his rank for them at every turn of the road.

One day the colonel was called to the Pentagon for a meeting. The next day he returned ecstatic. He had been promised a promotion to brigadier general and command of an overseas brigade of troops. He returned to the Gap to tie up loose ends, pick an official staff to accompany him, and ship his family back home. He called and asked me to accompany him as his Brigade Information and Education Officer and personal advisor. I would be promoted to captain before sailing.

We worked for weeks on the plans which were supposedly secret. Obviously they were not because staff officers whom the colonel did not pick to accompany him set out to destroy him and his future. Four weeks after he returned from Washington with his heart leaping with excitement over a promised generalship and a new command, Colonel Ambrose was sacked and sent into oblivion somewhere beyond reach of friends and opportunity. This man was punished because he dared to care and fight for the Black men under his command who could neither fight nor fend for themselves. He was one of the finest and most decent men I have ever known. I believe his defense of my programs aborted his career. I never saw the colonel again. Years after the war was over, I was startled to read in *The New York Times* of his death in a commercial airplane crash somewhere in the West.

Chapter Nine

Although Colonel Ambrose had left, my career was so closely tied to his that I knew I was a marked pigeon with the hunters just waiting for the right time to wing me. Colonel Ambrose's successor was the former executive officer who had undercut him and helped to mastermind his downfall. This commander was an arrogant, mediocre lawyer with a gigantic inferiority complex. He called me in for instruction and castigated me for past performances, and then warned me of sending me to "Siberia" if my "wild and woolly" lectures continued. A period of harassment set in that was difficult to believe. My headquarters telephone was tapped and counter intelligence men were inserted in my staff. The lieutenant in charge of social services and troop affairs with whom I had to work closely was assigned to shadow me so my every movement and statement were reported to the intelligence section of the post.

Now occurred an incident for which I risked my commission. One day all the bulletin boards in the white camp area had screaming posters announcing that Duke Ellington's band would appear for a big dance in an area where the Black troops could not even loiter. I raised hell because Duke was a Black idol, and to bring him to a camp where five thousand Blacks were stationed and deny them the right to hear him was callous and stupid. I lost. The rationale for this insulting episode was the military philosophy of "give the white troops the best." Ellington was not aware of the situation when he contracted to play. The Black troops became more restless and morale was lower than ever.

On the heels of this there arrived in camp the remnants of a dismantled Black tank destroyer battalion who had lost their combat designation and best officers, and were now converted into a stevedore battalion with unsympathetic white officers. They were ready to riot. I spent days and nights working to prevent a bloody confrontation. This new outfit was readied and shipped out in record time.

The commandant realized that the "Ellington affair" had left an open wound and he decided to bring a lesser band to the camp for an all-Black dance. I decided to prevent this event from coming off, because if it succeeded Black troops would always be treated to lesser opportunities and privileges.

The YWCAs in the cities around Indiantown Gap sponsored dances and social evenings for the Black troops in the camp. The Reading YWCA coordinated the collection and chaperoning of young ladies who were bussed to the camp as "dates" for a particular occasion. If the big dance the commandant was about to sponsor were to be a success, several bus loads of young women would have to arrive for the occasion. The Reading YWCA promised to deliver and plans went forward to make this a gala event.

A week before the dance I went to Reading to spend the weekend with friends, Dr. and Mrs. Lee Terry. They were prominent Black citizens in Reading and very active in all civic affairs. Under their auspices, I met many of the parents of the "dates" for the dance and secured their help in preventing the twelve bus loads of girls from unwittingly aiding and abetting the demeaning attitude underlying the commandant's dance. On the night of the dance, each company commander lined up his troops and marched them to the party site. Twelve hundred men stood waiting for the "dates." They never arrived! The troops raised hell and stomped out, leaving the band to play for itself and the thoroughly bewildered and confounded officer corps.

The Counter Intelligence Division started an investigation. They suspected me but did not have adequate proof. The commandant asked me what I thought had happened. I told him that the practice of subtle discrimination could be seen through even by simple Black troops. His dismissal of me was curt and angry.

The morale of the troops was at a point so low that it frightened me. Many of the white officers were castoffs from white outfits that didn't want them, and they were resentful and outraged to be serving with Black troops. They often acted like slave owners, and ran their outfits like plantation bosses. Some of these officers were slated for extermination when the troops arrived overseas.

One night, Captain William Bryant, now a Federal judge in Washington, D.C., and at that time one of the highest ranking Black officers, came up from Washington on an inspection mission to review my program. After dinner, as we were making rounds in the camp, we overheard a conversation among several soldiers. They were plotting to murder a very unpopular company commander, a man who treated his troops with contempt and insult. This officer is today a very important figure in the U.S. government and he still does not know that Captain Bryant and I saved his life by tactful handling of this band of plotters. We entered the barracks where the plot was being planned. Calling the troops to attention, we reminded them that any stupid plots against their officers would result in prison terms or even death. This kind of retaliation was counter-productive and insane.

On another occasion a frightened sergeant came in haste to my quarters one night to beg me to come to his barracks and disarm a ranting, raving soldier who was threatening to kill all the men in the barracks with his loaded carbine. Looking through the window of the barracks I could see this man sitting on a bunk in the center of the room. He was pointing his carbine at about thirty men lined up against the wall. I walked into the room, went straight to the soldier and requested the rifle. The only reason this maniac did not shoot me was because his feverish brain could still remember my efforts to help him and the others on that post. The system had reduced him to an unbalanced creature.

One Saturday afternoon Roy Wilkins of the NAACP and my good friend, Dr. Arthur Logan, flew from New York to visit me. They were aware of my desperate situation at the Gap and wanted to cheer me up and give me moral support. Their visit was a great boost to my shattered nerves and faltering spirit. Arthur arrived with news from his family that if I were court-martialed they would supply the funds to hire the best lawyers to defend me.

Each day the pressure became greater and the obstacles thrown in my path grew bigger and bigger. One day the officer in charge of troop affairs, Lieutenant Squires, whom I had known for some time was assigned to shadow me, phoned and asked me to stop by his office for a chat. Since he was also in charge of the officers' club, he always had on hand a good supply of whiskey. Feigning good fellowship and camaraderie, he proffered a drink. Then he began: "Fred, I want you to believe I'm your friend. My job brings me in contact with the brass every day so I generally know all the scoop. The latest is that you're in deep trouble, and you need friends to defend you at court. Now I believe I can help you if you come clean with me.

"First of all, the Old Man is still teed off about the dance. He says it was sabotaged and only you could have done it. He's still investigating and if you did it, it's curtains for you.

"Also, that organization you worked for before coming into the service—what do you call it—the advancement society?—anyway, the Old Man says it's a bunch of communists and you are taking orders from them. If he can prove this, you're on your way to Leavenworth for a long time.

"Now, why in hell don't you plead ignorance, and promise to stop baiting the troops and turning them against their officers? You can get a promotion and a good spot somewhere if you'll just confess that you did not know the gang you are working with are commies."

The language I used does not belong in this book, but in essence I called the lieutenant a "lame-brained son of a bitch" and told him to tell the general to go to hell.

The die was cast.

I called Thurgood Marshall, chief counsel for the NAACP and asked him to send me an NAACP letterhead at once. The letterhead contained all the names of the board members, and among them were two U.S. Senators, a Federal court justice, two U.S. Congressmen, and the wife of the President of the United States, Mrs. Eleanor Roosevelt.

About a week after I slammed Lt. Squires' door in his face and left his office in a fury, the call came from the head of camp security for me to go the commandant's office. I did not have to be told the reason. The stage was set for a human weenie roast! I walked in and saluted the general and, at his command, sat in a chair on his left facing five other officers. The trial was on. The general cited my record of "flamboyant" activity since coming to the camp: for example, the lectures that put a glint in the troops' eyes; incessant insistence upon recreational and social facilities for the troops; demands for more Black OCS candidates; crusading in nearby communities for support for Black troops; suspicion of sabotaging the dance; general attitude of aloofness and superiority; and communistic views. He accused the NAACP of being a communist organization and me of carrying out their orders. He said I was a menace to security and the U.S. war effort. What defense, if any, did I have?

I said: "Sir, this is not a duly organized court of law or court martial, and I am not compelled to expose myself to this military lynching. However, it does give me an opportunity to get on record as addressing myself in your presence to the damnable accusation that I am a communist, or that the NAACP is communistic and that I am representing them here in this camp. You have damned and condemned a lot of prominent and loyal Americans, Sir, among them the wife of the President of the United States. I confess that if she and the senators and congressmen represented on this letterhead are communists, so am I, for they approve and direct the actions and programs of the NAACP and its staff. I shall inform Mrs. Roosevelt tonight of your charges!"

I saluted and walked out.

Chapter Ten

Needless to say I was not court-martialed. I waited days for action. It never came. A month later, however, the general was shipped out of the camp. Some said he was "sent so far away that sunshine would have to be piped to him." I never knew where he went.

I knew the time had come for me to try to get a transfer quickly because the general's allies would try to vindicate his awkward failure. Besides, I wanted to see duty in the war zone because that was the ultimate reason for being in the Army in the first place.

Just about this time Colonel B.O. Davis, Jr., a West Pointer and the second highest ranking Black officer in the Army, returned from his 99th Fighter Squadron command in Europe to lead and train a new and larger Air Force group. It was to be the 477th Composite Group, made up of the 99th Fighter Squadron and the 617th and 618th Bombardment Squadrons.

Colonel Davis was the son of the sole Black general, B.O. Davis, a veteran of long service. General Davis did not have a command during World War II. Colonel Davis caught hell at the Point during his training there but he came through it with courage and high marks. He was a 'no-nonsense' disciplinarian, and his men and outfits were some of the best in the entire U.S. Air Force.

The original 99th Pursuit Squadron won fame and glory in Italy, and for the subsequent 477th Group only the brightest, best educated and most talented Black youths in the United States were chosen. These men etched a new era in U.S. war history.

Colonel Davis asked me to join the 477th Composite Group, which was to leave soon for the Pacific. I would serve on his staff as Information and Education Officer for the whole group. I accepted with alacrity and received orders to proceed to Godman Field, Fort Knox, Kentucky. After the ragtag outfits I had served with, it was an honest thrill to join Colonel Davis' command. I had never seen so many high-ranking officers, so many handsome, educated Black men, and so many dashing, competent pilots. I wished that every Black soldier could have the chance to serve in a first-rate outfit under trained, competent, experienced officers.

Colonel Davis was a tough taskmaster. He had to be. He was not going to fail, and his men, on parade at all times and holding the key to the military future of Blacks in their performance, had to excel. Moreover, the colonel was a career soldier, and despite his high rank he could not knock down all the barriers and hurdles in the path of Black soldiers. He did everything by the book, and no matter how distasteful a situation, a custom, or a procedure was, he handled it without complaint.

Sometimes this was hard to accept. For example, Godman Field was on the Ft. Knox Reservation, yet Davis' troops were restricted to the perimeters of the field and could get into great trouble if they tried to use the facilities at Knox. Davis' retort to a complaint of prejudice and discrimination probably would have been: "We are here to train for combat, not to socialize or crusade for civil rights." Even the railroad station on the post was segregated, and many brawls occurred at the bus station in Louisville because the Jim-Crow regulations were enforced by the white military police. I became involved in one incident and was nearly thrown out because of it.

Members of our military police unit were on duty at the Louisville bus station one cold winter night and tried to purchase hot coffee at the counter inside the station. The waitresses refused them service and ordered them to leave. It was the only place where coffee could be bought, but it was for whites only. Lieutenant Thernell Anderson, the officer in charge, then entered the station and politely asked if the lady in charge would provide coffee for the MPs to drink outside. She refused and called the sergeant of the white MPs on duty at the station and accused Lt. Anderson of insulting her. Lt. Anderson was roughly handled by the white MPs, beaten, arrested and carted off to the local jail. The local authorities notified Colonel Davis that Anderson had been jailed, but instead of asking for his immediate release, the colonel told the authorities to hold Anderson and he would send for him the next morning.

When the Black soldiers returned to Godman Field and told their comrades what had happened at the bus station, the whole outfit became incensed and angry at Colonel Davis for treating so casually the insult to Black troops and for being so insensitive to the plight of Blacks struggling to "soldier" under discriminatory conditions. Matters were no better the next day. Anderson was released and brought back to camp only to be given hell by the Colonel for breaking the southern social code by attempting to purchase coffee for his freezing men at a "for whites only" coffee bar in a sleazy, dirty bus terminal. On top of that, the Colonel said he was going to court-martial him for the "offense."

A committee was formed among the Black soldiers to draw up a petition to the colonel protesting this treatment and to begin work on his behalf in the event he was brought to court martial. Because of my affiliation with the NAACP, my help and advice were asked. I went to the executive officer and told him that if Anderson were punished I would request the NAACP to go to the War Department not only to cancel

Anderson's sentence, but to reprimand Colonel Davis for an action inimical to the interest and welfare of the men in his command.

I spent six months with the 477th Composite Group, but it became evident that we would never carry out our original mission of serving in the Pacific. The war was winding down. The war in Europe ended on May 8, 1945, and the atomic bomb was dropped on Hiroshima on August 6th. The handwriting was clearly on the wall. Only those interested in making a career of military service hung on. The rest of us were in a hurry to return to graduate school or other civilian pursuits.

I started making plans for my postwar career with great trepidation. I could return to my job at the NAACP, but with the GI Bill of Rights I had the possibility of realizing my old dream of studying law or trying to find a new role in business or industry. The latter proposition was only a hazy hope because old man Jim Crow was still alive and active, and he would try to block all attempts to escape the restrictions of segregation and discrimination.

I had come to the end of another traumatic period in my life. In the five days I spent at the mustering-out station at Fort Dix, New Jersey, I soberly reviewed the past four years. It was evident to me that I had matured into manhood in the service. I had chosen the road I would follow the rest of my life—the pursuit of equal opportunity and equal rights and justice for my race—and any others that came within my orbit. I had learned to despise injustice, segregation, discrimination and dishonest public servants. The system under which I had served four years was inhuman and unfit to be the system under which the United States purportedly fought and her sons died to spread democracy across the world. I must hasten to find another vehicle which might help me escape from the chains of status quo, and enable me to move the struggle for Black dignity and first-class citizenship one more mile down freedom road.

I left the service bitter and angry about the sacrifice of four years to ignominy and personal shame. I knew without contradiction that as long as I lived, I would never escape from America's shameful method of dealing with race and color.

Accepting this conclusion would for the rest of my life preserve my sanity, and prevent me from physically or mentally destroying my life by action or deeds of a demented or tormented man.

On October 1, 1946, I was mustered out of the Army with the rank of major and I entered Rutgers University School of Law on October 6th. I was thirty-six years old, the oldest man in the class where the others averaged twenty-five years of age.

Chapter Eleven

Maturity has its advantages. My sole drive in law school was to do well and get out as quickly as possible. If I attended classes all year, including summer, I could complete all the work in two years. This I did and graduated in September, 1948.

Law school was a stimulating experience for me. It gripped my imagination and I felt that I had at long last found a vehicle for success, as well as a weapon to use to defend Blacks against the inequities of the social and economic systems. However, there were still two hurdles to overcome before I could begin to practice. The first was a year's clerkship in an attorney's office and the second was the bar examination.

After graduation I spent six weary weeks canvassing law offices for a clerkship. None would accept me. There were fewer than a dozen Black lawyers in the whole state of New Jersey and most of them barely eked out an existence. There were two or three in Newark, perhaps two in Jersey City, and the others were scattered through south Jersey. They handled police court cases and an occasional real estate closing. At any rate, none of them was equipped to retain a clerk and the offices were often in the lawyer's hat rather than in a public office building. The scheme of life in New Jersey, as in many other states, did not provide for the entry of Blacks into the practice of law or into business or corporate life, and to prepare academically for such a career was done at one's own risk.

Just as I was ready to discard the whole program, a young Jewish lawyer in Englewood, Sidney Dincin, heard of my plight and offered me a clerkship in his office. He worked hard with me and together we poked into every facet of law past and present. Sidney was an able and conscientious counselor. He represented many impoverished and friendless citizens at the bar, and because he was a Jew he knew all the heartbreak of insult and denial and bigotry. Our friendship went back to 1932 when I petitioned to become a member of the Young Republicans.

No Black had been given membership in the Young Republicans before, and Dincin carried my fight to the floor of the Annual Convention at the Berkeley Carteret Hotel in Asbury Park, New Jersey. Finally, I was given permission to present my petition to the whole convention. When I arrived at the hotel, however, the hotel people would not permit me to enter because they had a policy against admitting Blacks to the hotel for any reason. May it always redound to the credit of the State Chairman, Albert B. Hermann, that the whole group immediately petitioned the governor of the state, Harold Hoffman, to send state troopers to the Berkeley Carteret to protect me and escort me to the podium to make my speech. It was probably the most ardent speech I ever made and resulted in opening the membership of the Young Republicans in New Jersey to Blacks and to my becoming vice chairman of the group.

Before taking the bar exam, a candidate had to appear before the fitness committee of his county bar group, after having presented the group with an application signed by five citizens testifying to the candidate's reputation, family background, and character. One of the signers of my application was a prominent Hackensack lawyer, Dominick Pachella, of immigrant Italian parentage. He had gone to high school with me and had made great marks in life by defending unpopular causes and poor clients with considerable success. My reception by the fitness committee was icy. The chairman held my application and scanned it as if it were a dirt-diseased scrap. His first question was: "How long have you known Pachella? Why did you have him sign your application? Are you aware that he is not held in high esteem by his peers? Are you a member of any group or organization he espouses? You were with the NAACP, weren't you? Do you intend to rejoin them?"

My pressure went to the boiling point. I was livid with anger. I told them that Pachella had been a loyal, decent, helpful friend for years. Discrimination against him had been almost as great as it had been against me, yet he had overcome all the obstacles placed in his path to become a lone legal centurian for minorities in Bergen County. I asked him to sign my petition because he was my friend and I was proud of him; if I could practice law in his mold I would be proud and grateful indeed. When the interview was over I knew I would never practice law in New Jersey.

Two days are required for the bar examination, which is given in Trenton. The Stacy-Trent Hotel was the customary place to stay. Along with a dozen of my law school classmates, I made a reservation and received a confirmation. We all arrived at the hotel about six o'clock the evening before the test. Despite the confirmation, there was no room for me in the hotel. The clerks disclaimed any knowledge of a reservation or confirmation and turned me out into the night with no place to go. These were not the days when one could approach a nearby parsonage and ask the minister for help. Here, on the eve of the greatest academic test of my life, I was adrift in the streets of a strange city like an outcast or a bum! I walked back to the railroad station I'd just left an hour ago, and there, dejected and panicky, I sat and tried to think of something to do. Bitterness and fury consumed me. I could not eat or read a newspaper. At last, hungry and weary, I started to walk the streets to find a place to get coffee and a roll. But it was the small hours of the morning and nothing was open.

Suddenly from the deep recesses of my mind emerged a name associated with Trenton. My brother John had taught briefly at the Bordentown Manual Training School in the 1930s, and in his effort to inspire and motivate Blacks he had served on social service committees with a prominent white woman, Mrs. Mary Emma Yard. John had told me that her grandfather Roebling built the Brooklyn Bridge and her mother was president of a Trenton bank. I took up courage in both hands and looked up Mrs. Yard's name in the telephone book at the railroad station and put through the call. A frightened woman answered the telephone and I quickly stammered out my name and John's and my apologies for calling and told her my plight. She gasped in disbelief and told me to get in a cab and come right to their apartment. She said my accommodations would have to be makeshift because they had a two-week-old baby who was sick with colic. But they had a couch in the den and I could sleep there.

I shall be eternally grateful to the Yards for their merciful hospitality. They were tired and worn out from being up with the sick baby, but at three o'clock in the morning they welcomed me with warmth, and even apologized for the couch. No one in that household slept those few hours before dawn, and when day broke I felt sick and exhausted. The Yards fixed me a grand breakfast and sent me on my way with a prayer for good luck and painful regrets for the inconsiderate treatment dealt me by the Stacy-Trent Hotel.

I will never know if I actually failed the bar examination. My anger and despair had left me almost irrational, and my tired, bloodshot eyes could barely focus on the examination questions. But Sidney Dincin and I had drilled and drilled on the fundamentals of law so long that I could recite them like a poem. Whether I passed the bar exam or not, I had to make a living. I had gone to law school on the G.I. Bill, and it did not cover actual expenses. My mother had to have continuous medical care and special foods, and while sister Nellie helped carry the brunt of this expense, I worked at odd jobs during evenings and weekends to make up the balance. It was an exhausting schedule.

Perhaps it was fortuitous at this moment of chaos and indecision that I was recalled to active duty as a reservist because of the situation in Korea. Black field-grade officers were not being sent overseas in great numbers, but apparently the military stance was being reassessed. I was ordered to the Artillery School at Fort Bliss, Texas, for a six-months' refresher course.

The Fort Bliss program was interesting and demanding, and it temporarily blunted the nightmare of the bar examination experience. The officers attending the school at Bliss were divided into classes. I was the ranking officer in my class of forty-eight members and became the class leader and overseer. Many of the young white officers were from the South and it was a new experience and discipline for them to accept me as their leader. However, it worked out well and I relished the opportunity for leadership and responsibility.

After the first sixty days at Bliss it was evident that most of us would not be sent to Korea but would finish the course and return to our home reserve units. This advance notice of our possible home assignment alerted me to the necessity of using the remaining weeks at Fort Bliss to explore future career opportunities. Where could a Negro of my qualifications and experience apply for a job in 1950?

Daily, after grueling hours in the field, firing, assembling or dissembling a 105 millimeter cannon, I would sit in my barracks after dinner and think and think and think about where to apply for work. The "Equal Opportunity Employer" had not yet been invented and except for teaching, preaching, or blue collar work, the possibilities were distressingly few.

Then, one night I remembered a gentle, kindly man I had met during negotiations at CBS Radio years before. We wanted CBS to carry a Duke Ellington concert across the country to celebrate the 40th anniversary of the founding of the NAACP. If a network would donate the time and facilities, Duke would donate his time, band and fees for an hour's broadcast. Various corporations would contribute to the expense of the hour with a brief announcement of their products, with a percentage of the cost going to the NAACP, which was in dire financial straits.

For weeks Gerald Maulsby and I worked together, thrashing out the details and securing the approval of the network.

Maulsby was thoroughly sold on the idea. He pushed it through and helped to make it a stunning success. I sat down and wrote a letter to Maulsby. I cited my dilemma and asked if he would be willing to sponsor my application for employment at CBS. The response was quick, and the answer was "Yes!" He told me to call him as soon as I returned from Fort Bliss and come to his office for a chat. I was ecstatic! It didn't guarantee a job, but it indicated that there were people of good will who do make an effort to assist their fellows.

Three months later I sat in Maulsby's office, chatting about my past, present, and future. He was a prince of a man and even though he said he was not a "big shot" at CBS, he was ready to use whatever influence he had to help me get an interview. Soon I received a call from the director of personnel, Mr. Kalaijian, to come and see him. The first surprise on entering Kalaijian's office was to see that he had a Black secretary, Anne Campbell. This was a rarity in 1950! This young lady was attractive, well-groomed, well-dressed, and able and competent as I later learned. Her presence told me something important and reassuring about Mr. Kalaijian. The interview lasted a half hour. Kalaijian seemed to be fascinated by my curriculum vitae and the verbal account of my life. He felt that I had the experience and stamina to undertake a "guinea pig" role at CBS and he would try to arrange it.

I would be interviewed by the division head and other senior officers and their decisions would determine my fate. A month later I became an employee of CBS as a "writer" in the Public Affairs Division primarily preparing feature stories and squibs about future television programs and events. I would have to sit at the feet of the master writers for six to nine months to get the hang of the business and if my tryout was successful I would become a regular staff member.

Chapter Twelve

It was like being in college again. This was a special kind of writing and it had to be clever, appealing, colorful, and subtle. It had to make people want to watch the program. Viewers are the lifeblood of television, and the competition among networks is tough and unremitting. People read reviews and commentary about coming programs to determine whether they will watch them or not. Their decision is often based on the description of the feature they read in *TV Guide*, the TV section of the daily newspaper, or a squib used as an advertisement on the TV screen.

I worked diligently spending long hours in the evening after work honing my mental tools. On weekends we were assigned specific TV programs to audit, not only on CBS but on rival networks. We needed to watch the opposition to make sure our product was superior to theirs.

The senior writers were jealous of their prerogatives and not all took kindly to the novice or journeyman who joined their profession. However, the division head, Hank Warner, a rotund, jovial man and a brilliant writer, took a liking to me from the start and he eased my path and problems with a savoir-faire that did not ruffle the feathers of less friendly staff members. Eventually, I was assigned as assistant to Beryl Reubens, an able and energetic writer of television features and news stories for the press and magazines. He had a flair for interesting and descriptive articles that helped increase the number of CBS viewers. This in turn increased the revenue from advertisers. Writers of this type are in great demand and receive top salaries. Some become eccentric prima donnas and give their staffs a hard time.

I wasn't accepted with open arms by everyone at CBS. Having a Black in a white collar job in the burgeoning television industry was a new idea. Those young whites who were making a niche for themselves in this new commercial bonanza were jealous of the opportunity it gave them and did not want strange new competition. However, this was just the kind of challenge I liked and functioned in well, so I waded in with determination.

No one achieves success solely through his own efforts. He is either helped by someone or has a lucky break. Hank Warner, the supervisor, and Beryl Reubens and John Horn, top feature writers, took a genuine interest in my efforts to learn the trade and overcome the myth about Blacks having difficulty in grasping the hang of a new, technical operation.

After ten months' apprenticeship I was gradually given opportunities to write short articles for the press about future TV programs and I sat in on meetings of the top writers when plans were made to handle feature stories of the reigning TV stars or when big political stories were about to break. It was a fascinating, completely absorbing existence. It was particularly refreshing to sit in studios where films were being made for the great TV series, "See it Now," or "You are There," narrated by the famed Edward R. Murrow. These stories were about great moments of history, past or present, and they were dramatized and brought to life on the TV screen by the leading TV actors and actresses of the day.

At the beginning of the second year, I was selected as a member of the Labor-Management Committee and became an editor of the CBS house organ. This detailed the problems of staff and management, discussed successes and failures, and outlined future goals and stories of general interest to people working in CBS-TV.

Television was just breaking upon the world so this was a fascinating and pulsating moment to be involved in any facet of its spread and development. For me the most intriguing element of this experience was to be hurled pell-mell into the intricacies of big corporate politics, to observe the decision-making and follow-through, and who was who and where in the pecking order. These are the politics of survival, the tools a pioneering Black especially must learn to use skillfully if he is not to remain forever a token figure. Often corporate bosses feel they have satisfied the spirit of cooperative human relations by putting Blacks at desks in the same room with whites, leaving them there to splutter and flounder until attrition solves their plight. I learned back in my crusading days at the NAACP that no one was ever going to hand Blacks opportunity on a platter. They had to be better qualified for the job and brighter than anyone else. Unfair? Yes, but the rules of the game are not promulgated by the minorities.

At CBS I watched with awe and fascination the ebb and flow of power. TV was a gigantic new medium of communication, destined to revolutionize the mores and life styles of millions of people throughout the world. Great giants like CBS, NBC, ABC and the others were battling for a share in the market, and for the greater profits that would accrue to the successful competitor. Colossal salaries were paid to those persons whose genius helped accomplish this and they were ordained leaders ad hoc. Their eminence was often of short duration because the least downward turn of the money graph brought in a new team.

Early in 1952 CBS was aflutter with great activity and preparation for TV coverage of the political parties' conventions and the national elections in November. Starting in January the political analysts and commentators were featured on prime time as they speculated on the party candidates. I was also assigned to audit programs of other networks to see how their coverage compared with ours.

The greatest speculation on all networks concerned the rumor that General Dwight D. Eisenhower would succumb to heavy Republican pressure and become the presidential candidate, leaving his post as president of Columbia University. What made this news sensational was the fact that until now Senator Robert Taft of Ohio had been assumed to be the front runner for the Republican nomination. The entry of Eisenhower would provide a rugged and hotly contested intra-party fight. It was all to be captured for TV.

I monitored the Republican Convention in Chicago in July, 1952. Endless hours were spent in front of my TV set checking CBS coverage and that of other networks, making sure that all vital aspects of this exciting and historic convention were captured for our viewers. The Republicans picked General Eisenhower and Senator Richard Nixon of California for their ticket, and Governor Adlai Stevenson of Illinois was the Democratic candidate.

Chapter Thirteen

I had not been politically active since I began working at CBS. In late August Val Washington, Assistant to the Chairman of the Republican National Committee for Negro Affairs, wrote me that he would be in New York on business and asked me to breakfast. He wanted my help in the coming campaign. He needed strong, able Blacks to help round up and influence Black voters to support the Republican ticket in the November elections.

Beginning with the Roosevelt years Blacks had become wedded to the Democratic party. The Democrats had fostered the Works Progress Administration, relief programs, and various other projects designed to ease the devastation of the Depression. For the first time in history in the WPA program, Blacks were permitted to serve in white collar jobs even though many facets of the administration itself were segregated. Relief programs fed and clothed the jobless and Blacks were grateful. It was understandable that Blacks rallied strongly to the Democratic banner. This allegiance continued under Truman but with less fervor.

At breakfast that morning, Val gave a succinct wrap-up of the history of the Republican party and its relationship with Blacks. He pointed out that yeoman efforts would have to be made to re-enlist Black support for the Republican Party if it were to make the most of the present opportunity to regain national power and the White House. He was to head the all-out effort. He also needed Blacks who would help him influence the leaders of the party and liberalize their thinking and platform if they were honest in their desire to have Black votes help secure a victory.

Val wanted to place a Black in every echelon of the party structure during the campaign, and he was insisting that the National Chairman, Leonard Hall, include a Black on General Eisenhower's campaign train with duties commensurate with those of the other staff members aboard. This, especially, was a radical thought to present to party leaders in 1952, and Val talked hard and fought hard to get approval for it. When the plan at last had been accepted by both the campaign committee and the candidate, Val knew he had to choose a person comparable in background and education to the men who were running not only the campaign train but great parts of the general campaign.

Before Val Washington left New York he asked me to think about the part I might want to take in the campaign and said he would call me in a week to find out if I would join him. I was happy at CBS in spite of the problems. There was a challenge in my job, and I hoped to parlay this opportunity into a successful career. But I could sense greater opportunity if I took part in the coming campaign. Eisenhower was a national idol and his administration might offer Blacks an opportunity to complete the task of emancipation begun by Lincoln nearly a hundred years before.

After considering the pros and cons for several days, I decided to ask CBS for a three-month leave of absence so that I could work with Val Washington and be assigned to Eisenhower's campaign train as an advisor and consultant to the candidate. My superiors at CBS granted the leave, hoping my affiliation at the fountainhead of the Republican campaign would enhance their coverage and access to lead stories and events.

A telegram from the Chairman of the Republican National Committee directed me to join the boarding party for General Eisenhower's campaign plane at LaGuardia Airport in New York on Labor Day, September 5, 1952.

Eisenhower was headed for Moline, Illinois, where he would make his first farm speech of the campaign. From there, by train, he would begin a two-week "whistle stop" tour of the Middle West.

I had no credentials other than the telegram, and my efforts to convince the security force at LaGuardia that I had proper business aboard the General's plane were futile. Only the chance passing of a newspaper man from the *Herald Tribune* who knew me and interceded on my behalf enabled me to get aboard. I knew no one on the plane and had to fend for myself. The plane was loaded with seemingly important people, and the air was heavy with conversation and cigarette smoke. Up front I could see the back of Eisenhower's head in the midst of aides. I made my way to the rear of the plane and sat down. No one spoke to me or asked my name or position. I sat and read newspapers and looked out of the window.

When we arrived in Moline, I piled into a bus marked "Press" and rode to a huge auditorium. Fifteen thousand people were waiting inside for the arrival of the Republican presidential candidate. General Eisenhower's speech was dull and uninspiring and I could see disappointment and dismay on the faces of many of the listeners. He stumbled over words and left sentences unfinished. The speech failed to come to grips with the points of vital interest to the people in the audience. I wondered how this candidate so ineffective in speech could fence on the public stump with Adlai Stevenson, the brilliant wordsmith, who was his able and popular opponent.

Now I understood an editorial that appeared in many of the Scripps-Howard papers on August 25th. It observed: ". . . Ike is running like a dry creek . . ." This editorial spoke for a wide segment of the party that feared the possibility of throwing away another chance to defeat the Democrats. Despite Ike's personal popularity, Stevenson's speeches were getting great press attention and editorial praise.

After the speech, Eisenhower invited his staff and the press to his private car on the campaign train for a nightcap. I followed and stood in a far corner observing the proceedings. He had changed into a lounging jacket, slacks, and slippers. He walked down the aisle shaking hands and receiving adulation from the crowd. Finally he reached me and said: "I guess you're the new man on the staff. Welcome! What did you think of the speech?" I faltered and hesitated trying to think how to reply. All around me were the wheels of the party—House Leader Joe Martin, Senate spokesman William Knowland of California, GOP Chairman Arthur Summerfield, and a host of others. They had all heard the speech. What should I say? I reacted as I had been brought up to do and sacrificed tact for honesty. "Sir," I said, "I do not think we answered the questions in the minds of the people out there tonight. I watched their faces intently and they left uncertain and disappointed." Eisenhower's face showed his shock. "Come with me," he snapped. Inside he took my hide off.

I realized what I had done. I had challenged one of the greatest war heroes of all time who was running for the greatest office in the world. I, a former Army major, had dared to tell a five-star general he had failed in a mission! Eisenhower questioned my cheek and the presumption to present an opinion counter to that of the political pros who ran not only his campaign but the Republican party.

Through my mind raced the thought that honesty is not always the best policy and that I would be asked to leave the campaign train at once. But I wanted to retreat with dignity, so I risked one more statement. "Sir, I represent the ordinary American citizen. If I can understand something either written or spoken, then it is certain that the ordinary man in the street will too. But I did not understand the speech tonight and it did not help the people out there understand what your administration would do to lighten their burdens. Words were spoken but not ideas. What they hoped to hear and learn, never happened. I apologize for my irreverence, but I thought you'd like to know."

Eisenhower's reaction was that of a great man. A softness came into his eyes and speech and his reply made me feel both humble and contrite. "Fred," he said, "maybe you've got something there. Maybe these politicians are pulling my leg. Maybe we'll have to do something about getting the message across."

Perhaps at that instant Eisenhower got a glimpse of my worth to the campaign. Out of the mouths of children and fools the blatant truth comes and perhaps the shock of a civilian plebe criticizing his oratorical effort piqued his curiosity. From this ragged beginning, I traveled every mile of the long campaign with him. By train and plane we covered over 30,000 miles and poked into every nook and cranny of the continental United States.

The campaign trail was speckled with annoying incidents caused by my race and color. Even after twenty-five years some of these still rankle. In Los Angeles the campaign entourage had a gala parade from the airport through the streets of the city to the Ambassador Hotel. Here we were to spend the night and the next day. The Eisenhower party pulled into the circular driveway of the hotel and the Secret Service formed a flying wedge to rush the Eisenhowers through the dense crowd into the hotel. The staff followed. When I reached the entrance, the doorman grabbed me and said, "No! No! You can't go in this way. Go around to the back!"

I thought I'd misunderstood him and pulled away and struggled to get inside the foyer. By this time the other members of the staff were already inside the private elevators and out of sight. Not knowing what floor we had been assigned, I went to the desk. There was much conferring and confusion and finally I was handed a key and directed to an elevator off the back of the main corridor. The room I entered was in the back of the hotel on a floor reserved for servants or chauffeurs traveling with their employers. It was small and narrow, with a single bed, a sink in the corner, and a 40-watt bulb in a ceiling light turned on by a string dangling over the bed.

Long practice has taught me how to handle these insults to

color and race. It would not have been helpful to raise hell in a crowded hotel and embarrass Eisenhower. I would cool off, think it through and then act when I could assess all the consequences. The solution when it occurred was classic in its simplicity. It was an established custom of the campaign staff to have cocktails before dinner in some member's room. This was a good way to avoid public scrutiny and inquisitiveness and have a quiet time before the next public effort. This was my night to be host. We had arrived about four in the afternoon and, sure enough, at five a call came from one of the staff, saying, "Where the hell are you? What about cocktails?"

I told him to gather everybody and come on to the back of the hotel. They did. When they saw the miserable room I'd been given, they were shocked. It was beyond their belief that it could happen right under their eyes to a member of General Eisenhower's staff. A delegation went to the manager's office and demanded a good room for me on the same floor in the front of the hotel where the rest of the forty staff members were quartered. If he would not do this the whole Eisenhower party would leave the hotel. There were ludicrous aspects to the solution of the drama. I was placed in the Bridal Suite! The cocktail party was a fabulous success and was personally supervised by the manager!

Later that evening I wanted to surprise my cousin, a retired Army officer who lived on the west side of Los Angeles. I wanted to take a taxi to his house but none of the cabbies lined up outside the hotel would take me. Finally, I telephoned my cousin to ask if he would drive over to get me. He could not believe I was at the Ambassador. He said its policy was so racist that Blacks did not dare attempt to stay there.

I had naively believed that California with its multi-ethnic population would be without discrimination in its public places of accommodation. I had also relaxed my guard while traveling with the presidential candidate. As a member of his personal party it did not occur to me that I would meet head-on that old devil "discrimination." But many times I did on those travels.

The incident in Salt Lake City was pathetically humorous. This city was notorious for its discrimination against Blacks.

During my NAACP days I had traveled there to work with the branch and the race problems were legion. The Mormons own the city and they have a complete aversion to Blacks.

Eisenhower was to speak in the mammoth Salt Lake City Auditorium that night. The meeting was scheduled for eight o'clock, and the staff was told to assemble in the Salt Lake City Hotel foyer at 7:15 sharp for the parade to the auditorium. I left my room at seven o'clock to go down to the foyer. An elevator would stop at my floor, the young woman operator would see me and shut the door in my face. One girl even screamed when I tried to step into the elevator. The Eisenhower party waited for me until 7:40, then Governor Sherman Adams dispatched an aide to my floor to find me. The aide had to "commandeer" an elevator to get me to the ground floor. There was another hassle when we reached the auditorium. I was listed in the program as a 'platform guest' but the local host would have none of that. Eventually I was seated on the platform behind a large potted palm!

Going into the Deep South aroused real concern in the campaign party for my safety. Senator Hugh Scott of Pennsylvania, recalling the incident in his book, *Come to the Party*, wrote:

". . . When Ike flew into New Orleans he started a 16-hour Mardi Gras of his own. With a bow to the Creole tradition, Canal Street sprouted buttons reading, 'J'aime Ike.'

"Mindful that Stevenson had been widely criticized in the North for staying in a segregated hotel there, we had a train waiting for Ike. We were still most anxious to avoid friction involving any of our Negro staff members, among them Fred Morrow, a successful CBS official who later became a White House advisor to President Eisenhower.

"As the Canal Street parade was forming, Governor Adams gave me my order of the day. 'No matter what car you're supposed to be in, you ride with Fred Morrow and if anyone lays a hand on him, I want you to hit, whoever he is, with all you've got.'"

In another southern city, as we walked into the auditorium, Mrs. Sherman Adams took my arm and said, "Let them say something about this and see how they fare!"

A different kind of incident in Kansas City, Missouri, enabled me to save the reputation of a very prominent political aide to General Eisenhower, and thereby avert a scandal. We arrived in Kansas City from the West Coast for a Friday night rally. It was decided to spend the weekend in the city and leave on Monday for New York. The campaign train stood on a siding inside the vast Kansas City station and served as our hotel. After a visit with friends in town, I returned to the train late Saturday night and saw a crowd of people around a man who was lying prostrate on the floor of the station just opposite the private entrance to our train. A glimpse told me that he was a key aide to General Eisenhower. He had obviously passed out from overindulgence. In the distance I could see the station police approaching, so I knelt down and using a fireman's hold draped the prostrate body over my shoulder and staggered down the steps to the train. A porter helped me undress the aide and put him in his berth. We applied cold towels to his head and forced black coffee down his throat until he recovered consciousness. At one in the morning, weary and exhausted, I fell into bed. Governor Adams had called a staff meeting for eight the next morning, and we all had to be present . . . or else. The inebriated aide was at the meeting, wan, drawn, and bewildered. He never said "thank you" that morning or at any other time, but he became a stalwart friend of mine throughout the Eisenhower years. His future action on my behalf was his silent way of acknowledging gratitude for my help.

In San Francisco the Eisenhower party stayed at the St. Francis hotel. We had an entire floor and the Secret Service Command Post was set up just off the bank of elevators. My room was about fifty feet down the hall from the Command Post. The night we arrived I had dinner with several staff members, three young women secretaries and four men. I returned to my room about ten o'clock, read the papers for a while, then turned off the light and went to sleep. Suddenly, at three in the morning, there was a violent crash at my bedroom door. Then there was a splintering collapse of the door and it caved inward and smashed against the inside wall. Three men burst into the room and one focused a spotlight into my face and then flashed it around the room. I sprang from my bed in bewilderment, and he said, "Oh, we apologize. This is the wrong room!" Neither the intruders nor the manager ever explained for whom or what this raiding party was looking, but they scared me to death. I know what the maneuver was about. When the security detail saw me go to dinner in company with attractive young women, they were peeved. And when some of the party returned to their rooms at two o'clock, radiantly "high," it fanned the animosity of the security detail and aroused their curiosity as to the whereabouts of the "colored guy." They found me in bed, asleep and alone. I never mentioned this episode to Governor Adams or to any other official of the touring group.

The campaign drew to a close. We had crisscrossed the continent several times by plane and train and I had seen America under auspices that made this experience historic and special. No Black man had ever served a presidential candidate in this manner nor been privy to the give and take inside the group which directs and orchestrates the scenario for the "making of the President."

I had traveled every step with Dwight David Eisenhower, but as late as two weeks before the end of the campaign I had not had the opportunity to get to know the real man. I told James Hagerty, the press secretary, that I would make two important campaign speeches before election night in which I would try to sell him to Black America. If they were to be successful, I needed to be able to talk with conviction. Hagerty scheduled me for a half hour with Eisenhower "to talk." We were riding along the Hudson River from West Point on a beautiful October day and the General was holding meetings in the observation car of the train.

A week before in my hometown of Hackensack, Eisenhower had addressed a rally on the Court House green. He drove to Hackensack from New York for the occasion and the chairman of the New Jersey Republican Committee had greeted him with a request to give his committee a fifteen minute audience to clear up a bothersome political item. The meeting was held in the Bergen County Court House. At the meeting the chairman upbraided Eisenhower for appointing me to his campaign staff without clearing it with the state committee. He said the committee was incensed because Morrow was a notorious troublemaker, a militant, a hell-raiser for Negro rights and opportunities. He would become a millstone around Eisenhower's neck. Eisenhower thanked the Committee for its gratuitous advice and said he was very pleased with the service Morrow had given him. Furthermore, it was none of their damned business who he appointed to his personal staff, and when it came to the point where anybody's committee could dictate his choices, he would cease to be a candidate. His statement to the committee was phoned to me by a friendly member. I was not with Eisenhower when he visited Hackensack. Governor Adams had sent me to the Midwest to clear up a problem out there. However, in his speech from the steps of the county Court House to 200,000 listeners that day, General Eisenhower praised "your local resident, Fred Morrow, who has given so much, so well, to my campaign." Donald Borg, owner and editor of the newspaper, called my mother at home to tell her what Eisenhower had said. She was delighted.

The first thing I did at the interview on the train was to thank Eisenhower for the opportunity to serve him, and for the kind and generous words about me in his Hackensack address. His reply was that that was the way he felt about the situation. For the next thirty minutes we sat looking out as the Hudson rolled by while he reminisced about West Point and what it had meant to him. He thought that without his appointment to West Point he might still be a struggling farmer trying to eke out an existence in Kansas.

We finally got down to the status of the campaign. I told him that my two impending speeches would try to sell him to Black America. I wanted to be able to talk with honesty and sincerity about what he represented and what we might realistically expect from his administration.

I reminded him of his testimony before the Armed Services Committee relative to integrating the United States Armed Forces. He opposed integration because ". . . the climate was not right . . . that the various services were not ready spiritually, philosophically or mentally, to absorb Blacks and

Whites together." The ensuing din from the American Blacks was deafening, and Black troops went through a trying and hectic period after the testimony leaked out.

Eisenhower had a hurt look on his face after I posed the question. He looked at me long and hesitatingly and then began his reply.

"Fred, your father was a preacher, was he not?"

"Yes, sir, and so was my grandfather."

"Did either of them ever teach or talk to you about forgiveness?"

"Yes, sir. I've listened to many sermons on this subject."

"Well," he replied, "that is where I am now."

"You know," he continued, "it only dawned on me a few months ago the possibly biased quality of some of my testimony at that time. Before I came home to testify, I called in all my field commanders for an opinion. To a man, they all vehemently opposed the idea of mixing the troops. They said it just wouldn't work—and the task at hand was difficult enough without the added problems of race and color."

"You know," he added, "I knew this question might be raised during the campaign, and I've thought about it many times in the last few weeks, and what has struck me forcibly in my latest recollection is the fact that most of my commanders had southern backgrounds, and this may have influenced their opinion. However, I am sorry and I hope you especially understand."

Eisenhower paused reflectively, looking out at the stately Palisades as the train raced down the Hudson. He turned back to me and said softly, "I learned the courage and the reliability of colored troops during the Battle of the Bulge where many of them died because of inadequate training or lack of knowledge about their weapons. But they answered the call at that desperate moment when we had to throw everything we had into the maw."

"But, General," I interrupted, "what were your own feelings about Black troops and integration?"

Again, the gaze at the passing scenery, and a long pause— "When I talk about my commanders having a negative opinion, perhaps my own beliefs were shaped early in my military career. After West Point, I was assigned as an instructor to a colored National Guard outfit in Illinois. I was young—right out of West Point—and impatient with incompetence and slovenly execution. I was a spit and polish officer, and I wanted the troops to measure up to West Point standards. I remember taking the Rifle Team to the National Guard competition one year and the team was pathetic and painfully incompetent. I was ashamed and embarrassed.

"It never occurred to me that these men in the past had not been properly trained or led—and that for years incompetent and indifferent officers had been assigned to them. I just assumed that colored soldiers responded that way and that they didn't have it in them to 'cut the mustard.' I'm afraid that association with colored troops early in my career may have unconsciously obscured any positive thinking on the matter for years."

I had been in conference with Eisenhower for almost an hour and his secretary was constantly handing him notes about his schedule. I had been able to get a pretty good picture of his mental state at this time on his testimony before the Congress and he was really seeking forgiveness for his historic faux pas of 1948. I could believe his explanation, and I thanked him for his frank and forthright answers to my equally difficult and personal questions.

I got up to leave, and he said, "I have to address the people of the college (Columbia) neighborhood in an open air meeting tomorrow night—and the neighborhood is so diverse in ethnic composition that I've been trying to decide how to open the talk."

"General," I volunteered, "why don't you get up and just begin with: 'My neighbors, it's good to see and welcome you here tonight . . . .'"

"Fine," he exclaimed, and shook my hand firmly and warmly before I left.

The campaign had wound down to its final day which was spent in Boston. A tired but enthusiastic staff returned to New York early on Election Day morning. The Boston meeting had been a glorious success and *The New York Times* and other leading papers predicted Eisenhower's election. As the staff departed from Grand Central Station at two o'clock that morning, we all planned to assemble at the headquarters in the Commodore Hotel at six that night to await the returns.

I had not been home in two weeks, and so I used the opportunity to go to Hackensack to see my family, planning to return to the Commodore in time to have dinner and settle down in the Eisenhower headquarters for the returns.

I arrived at the headquarters at dinnertime but could not get up to the floor of the headquarters because it had been sealed off. Between the time we had arrived in New York and the present time, the Secret Service had issued new passes for the Eisenhower staff, and no matter who you were, admittance to the headquarters was barred without the proper new pass. For some of us who had not been present all day at the hotel this was catastrophic!

The Secret Service had resorted to this procedure after discovering that someone had made scores of counterfeit passes for admission to the headquarters to witness the election returns. It would have been impossible to screen all the new and unknown persons—hence the wisdom of canceling old passes and issuing new ones.

I was devastated by this turn of events. This night was the one all of the staff had been working for and looking forward to celebrating together. We were certain that General Eisenhower would win, and all of us wanted to be present for that historic moment of victory on November 4, 1952. Eisenhower swept the country. He carried 39 states including some in the South, won the electoral vote 422 to 89 and the popular vote by a plurality of 6,621,242. For the first time since 1928, a Republican had been elected President of the United States.

Chapter Fourteen

During the campaign I had neither discussed nor intimated to anyone any interest in a job in the new administration. Perhaps one reason was my lack of knowledge of how one would go about such a move. I was new to this business. Others, with influential Republican contacts, had etched out plans for rewards after the victory, but it just never occurred to me that I could aspire to such a position. However, Val Washington, the Black executive at the Republican National Committee who had had me placed as a campaign aide in the first place, was determined to have me and other qualified Blacks in the Eisenhower Administration. He laid careful plans during the campaign, and after the election pushed his demands. He wanted me in the White House!

While most of the Eisenhower assistants had gone on "rest vacations" right after the election, I had returned to my job at CBS Television. It was there in my office one day that I received a telephone call from Sherman Adams to come to see him at the campaign offices in the Commodore. The transition team was hard at work planning staff and other assignments, and General Eisenhower had appointed Governor Adams as his Chief Executive Assistant in charge of operations. Succinctly, Adams said: "Both the general and I like you, and were satisfied with the help you gave during the campaign. The general has asked me to offer you a job on the White House staff." I stammered thanks, and promised to see Governor Adams again within a week with an answer.

In my mind, CBS had offered me an opportunity to aspire beyond the normal confines of Black aspirations, and I had envisioned myself eventually climbing the corporate ladder to a really responsible place in the hierarchy. True, it had never been done before—but I'd planned to give it the "old college try." Going to Washington would mean a complete overturn of the current normalcy of my life. Besides my daily job, my present preoccupation was with the health of my invalid mother with whom I lived and cheerfully supported daily. She was diabetic and rheumatic, needing constant medical and nursing care. My sister, a school teacher, lived nearby and she ran in daily after school to supervise and lend a hand. However, I knew I could not leave without assuring that mother's comfort and care would continue.

Also, I was not a politician—merely a citizen vitally concerned about good government and the character and ability of those elected to administer it. I had hoped some day to run for Congress—but serving as a Black functionary in some administration did not cause the adrenaline to flow with vigor. On the other hand, what a fantastic offer and chance this was. I'd be the first Black in history to be an aide to the President of the United States! What an opportunity this represented to help italicize in a high place the plight of the denied, denounced, disenchanted, and devasted Black race!

I returned to see Governor Adams a week later with my answer. "Yes," provided the job offered was not a "token" carved out for a Black presence on the White House staff. I wanted to be respected as an able and capable person, who, though incidentally Black, could do a job of the same quality as any other individual recruited for the President's staff. I trusted Governor Adams implicitly. For the three months on the campaign train, he had been a kind although demanding friend. We had both tested the other and each instinctively knew the other was his kind of man.

Governor Adams told me to tender my resignation to CBS and get ready to go to Washington a week before the inauguration. He made appointments for me to see two or three persons (top corporate executives advising the General on the composition of the White House staff) and he said all future communication would be with his assistant, Maxwell Rabb. I informed CBS of the offer from Governor Adams, and gave three weeks' notice with my resignation. My colleagues at CBS were ecstatic about the opportunity given me, and to accent their enthusiasm, gave me a going away party and a gift for my new office.

I spent the last two weeks at home tidying up affairs and freshening my wardrobe. During this period, because the small town was abuzz with rumors and gossip about the inquiries of the FBI, I was aware of their full investigation of my life. In a small town like Hackensack, federal investigators can cause a furor because friends asked questions about a prospective appointee can read into the questioning any motive they wish to espouse. Hence, in the local barber shops, churches, and Black social circles, it was suspected that the Reverend Mr. and Mrs. Morrow's son Fred was on his way to the Federal penitentiary for some clever, dark deed he had pulled off.

Adams and the principal staff appointees had gone to Washington a month before the Inauguration to prepare for the transition, hence, communication with knowledgeable members of the Eisenhower group was impossible. There was the usual pre-inauguration confusion and no one had any answers or knew where they could be obtained.

I became anxious. Even ten days before the inauguration I still had not heard a word from Maxwell Rabb or Governor Adams. I had resigned from CBS, made plans for my mother, and was currently living on my meager bank account. I was also embarrassed because I could not talk about "going to Washington" or the details of my job or residence. All this aided and abetted the rumors that I was about to be sentenced to prison.

Two days before the inauguration, I went to Washington to confer with Val Washington. Val had been espousing my cause with sincere skill and vigor and he had a concrete promise from the party that I would be on the White House staff. However, up to this date, he could get no information on what was happening and we both sat in his office before Inauguration Day bewildered and defeated.

Val Washington had secured a good seat for me to attend the swearing-in ceremony on the east steps of the Capitol. There, before massive crowds, Chief Justice Fred M. Vinson administered the oath to Vice-President Nixon. Minutes later, with both the historic Bible that had been used by George Washington and Eisenhower's from West Point days, the new President took the oath from Justice Vinson.

I sat at the ceremony chilled, depressed, and heartbroken. I had worked hard and faithfully to get to this point and had anticipated sharing this ceremony with a chosen few to return to the White House for another historic moment as "the first Black man" ever to serve a President of the United States as an executive assistant. Instead, here I sat on this chilly day of January 20, 1953, a mere jobless spectator who would return home forgotten and humiliated.

After only three months of "politicking," the vagaries of this unpredictable vocation had laid me low. I was like a beached whale—high and dry on the sands of unemployment and with a loss of face. I could not return to my old job at CBS after such a dramatic exit a few weeks before. Likewise, it was obvious to neighbors and friends that something, or someone, had stymied my Washington arrival.

I decided to fly to Washington to talk with Val Washington and to discover what had happened. I was heartsick, embarrassed, and angry. It was incredible to believe that Governor Adams and the President could have willfully gone back on their promise to me of a job on the White House staff.

Val Washington was a tower of strength and encouragement. He probed and probed and probed and he requested from the hierarchy of the Republican National Committee an answer. One thing of great importance that Val came up with was that the FBI investigation uncovered nothing derogatory in my life and gave me a clean bill of health. This left only one deduction—that someone of great prominence and power had blocked the appointment. Meanwhile, I had to find a job, and they were scarce items for an educated Black in 1953.

Washington's relentless job campaign for me continued and he did succeed in embarrassing the administration into looking for a job for me. Six months later, in July, with the assistance of Charles Willis, Jr., assistant to Sherman Adams, I was finally offered the position of "Advisor on Business Affairs" in the Department of Commerce. It was a new position and a policymaking one of prestige and authority. At least it would put me on the Washington scene.

This was a pioneering job, and I had to convince a great many people in the Department of Commerce that it was possible to place Blacks in responsible government positions and have them measure up. In this respect, however, I was lucky. Charles Honeywell, Administrator of Business and Defense Services, and Sinclair Weeks, Secretary of Commerce, stood by me at every turn in the road and I began to etch out a niche for myself in this WASP bastion.

As appealing as the Commerce job appeared, it was not enough. Every day at lunch I would stroll by the White House and wonder what dramas were unfolding inside. I read daily of the comings and goings of the staff and regretted the omission of my name. I also spent endless hours with Val Washington, musing, probing, and theorizing. He used every opportunity he had to keep this unresolved riddle before the prominent men of the National Republican Committee.

While at Commerce, I made several trips across the country to speak at college graduations—or serve on panels at corporate conferences discussing problems of U.S. business. I always seemed to be a novelty at these affairs as well as in the Department of Commerce itself.

My complete preoccupation with trying to find a decent place to live in Washington kept my nerves ragged and my heart disconsolate. Jim Crow was at its height in Washington in 1953 and its laws and customs dampened any enthusiasm from a good and challenging job. Daily I would take the "colored section" of the Washington Post, hire a car, and check out each ad describing a "comfortable, pleasant room" in a Black neighborhood. Each day, I would see only dingy, dark rooms with worn rugs and furniture in desolate neighborhoods. One day, I thought I had found an exception, when I stepped into a two-room apartment with fireplace and cheerful decor. While inspecting the fireplace, a large rat jumped out and ran across the room to a hole behind a sofa! I exited with alacrity.

No Black shopping downtown could stop at a soda fountain or an eatery for a meal. Blacks could only eat at a Jim Crow section in Union Station. One could only ride in "colored cabs" if available or attend "colored movies" in colored neighborhoods. Every facet of life was ordered and controlled—a maddening atmosphere for any citizen who pledged allegiance to the flag, sang "The Star Spangled Banner," and believed the immortal words of the Constitution of the United States. It was in this setting that I "hunkered down" in Washington in 1953 to keep watch along the Potomac for my White House opportunity. It might never come, but I would have to know why.

My job went along well considering that the department had never had to deal with a Black executive at top level. At points there were schemes, foot-dragging and attempts to thwart and sabotage—but I did not fall or lose my poise.

At a pre-Christmas staff meeting of top assistants, Secretary Weeks asked me to say a few words about my past months in the department. In the course of my remarks I thanked those who had readily extended the right hand of fellowship to me upon my arrival—and remarked that I found both interesting and challenging my continued role in the Eisenhower Administration as a "guinea pig." The remarks appeared to be well received. As a matter of fact, Weeks in his enthusiasm sent a copy of my remarks to President Eisenhower. A week later, I was stunned by a letter from the President extending congratulations on a job well done. He stated ". . . you are indeed not a guinea pig—but a highly respected and able American who has and is serving me well." This letter lifted my spirits as high as the Eiffel Tower and thrilled me to know the President was still aware of my existence and competence.

By July 9, 1955, I had been in Washington twenty-two months. It was a Friday and the usual hot, muggy weather persisted. I had planned to take the four o'clock train, the "Congressional," to New York and spend the weekend at home with my sister. My mother had passed away in September, and Nellie and I were still trying to pull things together and close the family home.

About 9:00 A.M., I got a call from Sherman Adams's office at the White House to report to him right away. Any summons from Governor Adams was ominous and the call was upsetting. On the way to the White House I searched my mind for any trespass, failure, or faux pas—but could think of none. Even so, I arrived at the West Gate a nervous wreck.

The guards at the gate made me furnish credentials and, ascertaining that I was the person the governor had summoned, opened the gate of the West End Drive visitors' entrance. Mr. Simmons in the visitors reception room checked me out again and then assigned a Black messenger to escort me to Adams's office.

A secretary ushered me into the governor's working office and without greeting or introduction Adams said: "It has been decided to bring you on the White House staff. The President has directed me to take care of all details. You will be Administrative Officer for Special Projects. Charlie Willis (Adams's assistant) will explain all the details to you and Andy Goodpaster (Colonel Andrew Goodpaster, White House staff secretary) will assign you an office. You will report at 8:00 A.M. Monday. Meanwhile, I'll call Sinclair Weeks and tell him you are leaving Commerce. Welcome aboard and good luck!"

With that phrase, I was dismissed and in a daze stumbled out of the governor's office at the side of Charlie Willis. I had waited two years for this call. It had come without warning or preparation, and I was almost paralyzed by its reality.

I arrived in New York about 7:00 P.M. and took a taxi home. As the cab was speeding north on Madison Avenue, the radio blared the news of my appointment, ending with ". . . the first Negro ever to be named to a presidential staff in an executive capacity." When the cab driver turned around to say, "Did you hear that?" he found a passenger with tears in his eyes.

Chapter Fifteen

Sherman Adams's bolt-out-of-the-blue message left unanswered the gnawing question of what caused the two-year delay. I knew better than to ask at this hectic time, but resolved to find the answer some future day.

The Sunday papers carried the story of my appointment to the White House Staff. The official news story carried a July 9, 1955 dateline and included the following text:

IMMEDIATE RELEASE   JULY 9, 1955

MURRAY SNYDER
ASSISTANT PRESS SECRETARY
- -

THE WHITE HOUSE

Everett Frederic Morrow of Hackensack, New Jersey, will take office Monday as Administrative Officer for the Special

Projects Group in the Executive Office of the President. Mr. Morrow has been, since September 14, 1953, Advisor on Business affairs on the staff of Secretary of Commerce Sinclair Weeks. In that capacity he served as liaison between the Commerce Department and other Federal agencies on programs designed to stimulate business growth and stability.

In his new post Mr. Morrow will be responsible for coordination of internal management affairs in the Special Projects Group which includes the Council of Foreign Economic Policy, headed by Joseph M. Dodge, the offices of Harold E. Stassen and Nelson A. Rockefeller, Special Assistants to the President, and the office of Major General John S. Bragdon, (S.S.A. ret.), Special Consultant on Public Works Planning. Mr. Morrow's office will be in the Executive Office Building.

He went to the Commerce Department from the Columbia Broadcasting System where he served on the public relations staff and as a member of the Employee-Management Committee. Prior to that, he was field secretary for the National Association for the Advancement of Colored People.

During the 1952 Presidential campaign, he served on General Eisenhower's campaign train as a consultant and adviser.

Mr. Morrow comes from a family long identified with the educational and civic development of Negro life. His paternal grandfather, Dr. John S. Morrow of North Carolina (an ex-slave), was a prominent educator and Presbyterian Minister.

Mr. Morrow was born in Hackensack, New Jersey, the son of the Reverend and Mrs. J. Eugene Morrow. He was educated in the Hackensack public schools, Bowdoin College, and Rutgers University School of Law.

He has been associated with the Social Service Federation of Englewood, New Jersey, and with the National Urban League as business manager of Opportunity Magazine.

In 1937 he became field secretary of the National Association for the Advancement of Colored People, and except for his tour of duty with the Army from 1942–1946, held this position until October, 1950. In 1951 he joined the staff of the CBS Network in New York City.

Mr. Morrow entered the Army as a Private in October, 1942 and was discharged as a Major in 1946. He is a Reserve Major of Artillery.

Monday morning I arrived at the White House West Gate at 7:45. Governor Adams had directed me to be in his office at 8:00 A.M. sharp. I gave myself plenty of leeway so as not to be late.

It is difficult to explain my awed feeling as I walked through that austere northwest gate of the White House on my first day of work. I was nearly emotionally overcome by the severe reality of the moment, and my mind was tumbling with thoughts of implications. I was leaving the privacy of my personal life to become public property. From this point on, the glare of public attention and observation would never cease.

The White House had arranged a swearing in ceremony and at 8:15 the Governor came out of his office and told me to follow him. We went over to the Executive Office Building to a conference room. There was a babble inside the room. There were present a dozen newspaper men and press photographers, as well as ranking White House staff members. Also, Val Washington, and my Congressman, William Widnall from New Jersey's 17th Congressional District.

I advanced to the center of the room, raised my right hand and placed my left on a Bible, and a White House clerk gave me the oath.

Adams was the first to congratulate me.

We lingered only a few minutes for others to gather round and wish me well and we were off to the office of the staff secretary, Colonel Andrew Goodpaster, to officially check in.

Goodpaster was a much decorated officer of World War II, a West Pointer, and a Princeton Ph.D. His greeting was warm with a firm handshake. He outlined my responsibilities as coordinator of internal management affairs in the Special Projects Group. I would be reporting to Colonel Goodpaster for the present, but with direct access to Governor Adams.

Wishing me good luck and offering any assistance I might need to get acclimated, Colonel Goodpaster accompanied me across the court to Suite 224 in the Executive Office Building. He opened the door and said: "This is your office—I wish you well."

Suite 224 is one of the finest offices in the government. On the second floor of the old State Department building, adjacent to the White House and connected by a ramp, it was one of the major suites in the old State Department hierarchy. Its architecture is superb—gigantic rooms with twenty-foot ceilings and everything done in oak paneling, offset by heavy office doors with beautiful brass knobs. It had an open working fireplace with brass accoutrements. The mantle over the fireplace was twelve feet long and ideal for the display of memorabilia. The furnishings were genuine English leather and the piece-de-resistance was the discreet but very adequate bathroom inside the working office. The outer office for secretaries gave an impressive entrance to the suite.

I walked into the inner office and plunked down into the "judge's" chair behind a huge glass-topped desk and stared at the buff-colored walls, bereft of pictures or decorations. My thoughts rushed about pell-mell. Here I was, amid all the trappings for a big man on the staff of the President of the United States. My surroundings suggested power and prestige and activity; yet no one had indicated how to get started to carry out the responsibilities just placed upon me. Where is the staff? Where are the blueprints on office procedure to follow? Where do I go to lunch? How do I approach the top assistants of the departments I am responsible for coordinating? Do I just walk into Nelson Rockefeller's office and introduce myself? If the telephone should ring, how do I answer it? What do I do with the pile of mail just dumped outside on a secretarial desk? God! Just what do I do?

At Officer's Candidate School during the war years, I had been taught that indecision is fatal in any battle. Decide! Even if it is the wrong decision—decide!

There were two telephones on my desk—a black and red—and I did not know which one was for what, but I chose the black one and asked the operator to get me the head of personnel. A woman answered and I requested the opportunity to talk with someone about my staff requirements. She would send an assistant over to see me. Twenty minutes later, a diffident young man appeared and asked, "What's the problem?" I pointed to my empty office and told him I'd been charged with a big and difficult assignment and needed staff assistance. However, for the moment, the most urgent need was an efficient and knowledgeable secretary. He winced when I mentioned a secretary. He wondered if I was high enough on the totem pole to have one—and maybe a day or two after I got started, I could run the shop alone.

I didn't surrender. I'd been in the Commerce Department and I knew what ranks got secretaries. I was only one step from the highest civil service rating in government and deserved not only a secretary but all the staff back-up my duties required.

He took another tack. What kind of secretary did I want? I understood the underlying meaning of the question. The White House had never faced the dilemma of having a Black, so staffing my office appeared to be a real problem. There were no Black secretaries or other staff members available. Would this mean selecting whites for this office? Wouldn't this create havoc in the White House stenographic pool—and generally in other pools throughout the civil service area from which other staff members would have to be recruited?

I faced the questioner head-on. "The only kind of secretary I want is an efficient and experienced one. One that you would select for Governor Adams's office. I don't give a damn if she is tall or short—black, white or yellow—pretty or ugly—bowlegged or long-stemmed—I just want a secretary from your White House secretarial pool!"

The man rose to leave; he was milky white around the gills and fire red around his ears. "Mr. Morrow," he said, "this will not be easy—I can't promise anything." And he left.

This was the first storm warning that Ole Man Jim Crow had followed me right to the White House and that the tour was going to be rough. The glow in my soul I had felt an hour ago when I took the oath was gone and I was back on the NAACP staff fencing with discrimination and segregation in the South.

Chapter Sixteen

I sat in my office several days alone, trying to overcome red tape and inertia and foot dragging in government agencies with which I dealt. No one had come forward to help me establish my office, or provide draperies or office equipment or manuals. Every day I'd call personnel and get the same response: "We're sorry, no one is available yet."

I could not protest to Sherman Adams, or Colonel Goodpaster. This may have been part of the test to see if I could take the gaff. However, I was determined that my office would be staffed and maintained, and would function like any other office in the White House. This would never be "the colored office" down the hall.

So far, all those offered a job in my office by their supervisors had refused. No one wanted the onus of working for a Negro boss. This was not said this bluntly, but . . .

July 15, 1955 was a banner day in my life. It started out like all the other days I had spent in the White House so far. However, late in the afternoon, I was sitting in the inner office, brooding on my fate, when there was a soft knock at the door. I opened it to find a shy, timid girl standing there. She asked if I were "Mr. Morrow." She kept the door open behind her, as if for protection and refused to come in to sit down. She literally blurted out her mission.

Her name was Mary O'Madigan. She was from Massachusetts. She was a member of the White House stenographic pool. Impelled by a sense of Christian duty, she had come to volunteer to serve as my secretary. She was aware of the attitudes of the other girls in the pool, but she felt she could not be true to her faith and condemn me simply because of my race. She wanted to try. I was overcome. The girl was crying!

From the day Mary O'Madigan entered my office, she became the keystone of its operation. This twenty-year-old, a graduate of a Massachusetts high school and a good secretarial school, had been in the White House secretarial pool for six months. Her secretarial skills were exceptional. In addition, she had a good mind, and she could anticipate what I would need, or have to do, or should do, in the exacting demands of my job. She was loyal and honest. She was not afraid to defend what she decided was right as dictated by her New England conscience. I could not have had a better friend and loyal ally than this young woman.

Mary immediately set about organizing the office. She knew where to call to get what was needed, and she handled the telephones expertly. In ten days she had secured office machines, stationery, messenger service, and drapes for the tall windows. She had an official car ready for me to use and had set up a schedule for me to meet and talk with the senior assistants in the programs which I was to coordinate.

I had not been on the White House staff for many weeks before I realized that I was to be a "whipping boy" for the Black press. This group expressed the frustrations of all Blacks as they tried to get attention and help with their myriad problems. It was universally expected that, with a Black on the President's staff for the first time, it would be easy to keep the

President informed of the vicissitudes of American life faced by Blacks and of Blacks' attitudes and reactions to their problems. The corollary to this was that, once informed by his Black aide, the President would act at once to correct the problems.

There was no visible evidence that the Administration was remotely concerned. Alone in my office I had to admit that the Administration was treating the Civil Rights issue as if it were an unpleasant phenomenon, to be avoided.

But the struggle for civil rights was heating up. After the Supreme Court's 1954 decision in the case of Brown v. Topeka, which reversed the old "separate but equal" schools decision of 1896, economic and physical reprisals flared all over the South. Blacks were fired from jobs and killings multiplied as whites fought the NAACP's drive for school desegregation and voter registration.

By 1955 the South was in a state of racial turmoil. White Citizens Councils, sponsored by Mississippi's most influential citizens in Senator James Eastland's home county, took the place of the Ku Klux Klan in support of the social and economic patterns of the white South. Eighty-five Dixie congressmen signed a manifesto called "Warning of Grave Dangers" that said protecting civil rights by legislation constituted a threat to liberty.

Then the Till case burst upon the country. Till was a fourteen-year-old Black boy from Chicago who was visiting relatives in Mississippi. He was accused of whistling at a white woman in a store and his trussed and mutilated body was found in a river. The Till case shocked and angered Black America.

Roy Wilkins of the NAACP pointed angrily at Eisenhower's silence on these issues and sent me a scorching note pointing out the Administration's responsibility to avoid "what could be an ugly racial conflict." Sacks of mail were brought daily to my office berating the President for his failure to denounce the breakdown of law and order and accusing me of "Uncle Tomism."

On November 29, 1955, I sent the following memorandum to Maxwell Rabb, Secretary to the Cabinet:

PRESIDENTIAL ASSISTANT
E. FREDERIC MORROW
TO CABINET SECRETARY MAXWELL RABB
November 29, 1955
(Morrow Files, Eisenhower Papers.)

The killing of the young Negro, Emmett Till, in Mississippi this fall, has received official attention from this Administration through the Office of the Attorney General. Under normal circumstances, this would be enough to satisfy most people that the police arm of the Federal Government was alert to all situations where possible Federal laws have been violated. However, this particular situation is so fraught with emotion because of the circumstances under which the crime was committed, and the fact that the victim was a youngster, that the normal methods of dealing with the usual case of crime are not completely acceptable to all of the interested parties.

There are visible indications that we are on the verge of a dangerous racial conflagration in the southern section of the country. The one theme on the lips and in the minds of all Negroes is the injustice of the Till matter, and the fact that nothing can be done to effect justice in this case. The warning signs in the South are all too clear; the harrassed Negro is sullen, bitter, and talking strongly of retaliation whenever future situations dictate.

It is a well-known fact that Negroes in Mississippi have formed an underground and are determined to protect themselves by methods that, if used, can only lead to further terror and bloodshed.

On the other hand, a frightening power has been built in Mississippi by the anti-desegregation White Citizens Councils, and their principal method is one of economic terrorism. These Councils are fanning out throughout the South, and they have created a climate of fear and terrorism that holds the entire area in a vise.

As a member of the White House Staff, I am sitting in the middle of this, and I have been accused of being cowardly for not bringing this situation to the attention of the Administration, and requesting the President to make some kind of observation on this unwholesome problem.

I feel the time has come when it might be advisable for Governor Adams or Vice-President Nixon to invite to

Washington a dozen of the prominent Negro leaders in the country and sit down with them to exchange views on this very dangerous problem. It will not be a matter of committing the Administration to any action it cannot take, but it will be a demonstration to the whole country that the responsible leaders, white and Negro, have a deep concern about this situation, and wish to sit down and talk about it intelligently and dispassionately. There is precedent for this kind of meeting, for, in my lifetime, it happened several times with Presidents Hoover, Roosevelt, and Truman. Meetings of this kind always have a steadying effect upon responsible Negro leaders, for they are able to go through the country and assure Negro citizens that the head of the nation is concerned about their welfare and will utilize the prestige of his office to prevail upon all to exercise common sense and common decency in dealing with the problem. By the same token, it notifies any racist element that the Administration frowns upon their un-American tactics, and will use the Office of the Attorney General to bring to justice any infractions of federal laws.

I would be happy to sit down and work out a list of invitees for such a meeting and I feel that time is of the essence.

A few days later, Rabb called me to his office and gave me a tongue-lashing on the Blacks' attitude. He pointed out that the President in his State of the Union message had suggested that a Congressional committee be appointed to survey the whole problem of civil rights and come up with recommendations for action. Rabb said that in view of what the Administration had done in this area Blacks were not demonstrating any kind of gratitude and most of the responsible White House officials had become completely disgusted with the whole matter. He said that Blacks were being too aggressive in their demands and that ugliness and surliness were showing through. He felt that the leaders' demands were intemperate and had driven most of the liberals to cover. He said that the Blacks had made no effort to carry along with them the white friends they had made and that he was afraid those white friends were becoming few and far between. Then he added that he had stuck his neck out in this matter before, and while he would always be for what was right, he could no longer argue that Blacks were a political asset or that doing things for them would gain any support for the Administration.

This meeting with Rabb brought into clear focus for me the impossible task I had assumed. I was an appointee who had sworn to serve the President and my country honestly and to the best of my ability. I was also a Black keenly feeling the ills afflicting my race, many of which I had suffered from. I was morally responsible to explain to American whites at the highest level of government what Blacks felt as they strove to secure the rights and responsibilities of citizenship that had been denied them for over three hundred years.

Despite Rabb's resentment at the raucous and constant prodding by Blacks on the matter of civil rights, incidents highlighting the issue multiplied daily. The South was a cauldron of racial strife and confusion in the early weeks of 1956 and in this critical election year the problem of color and race became a political football. Adlai Stevenson, the Democratic presidential candidate, was already capitalizing upon the silence of the Administration on civil rights. He skillfully proposed that President Eisenhower call a meeting of southern white and Black leaders in an effort to allay mounting racial tensions.

In a memorandum to Governor Adams on December 16, 1955, commenting on the Till case and conditions throughout the South, I recommended that a conference of a dozen or more leading ministers, Black and white, be called together under the auspices of the Administration to discuss what should be done. I suggested inviting ministers rather than lay persons to avoid giving such a conference a political cast or of appearing to endorse a particular philosophy on race relations. My suggestion was vetoed by higher authorities in the White House.

Early in February of 1956 two days of rioting broke out at the University of Alabama when the university defied a court order and prevented a young Black woman, Miss Autherine Lucy, from enrolling. About the same time in Montgomery, Alabama, an elderly woman, Mrs. Rosa Parks, tired after a day's work refused to transfer to a rear seat in the customarily Black section of a bus. She was brutally handled and then arrested. Little did we realize at the time the historic proportions of this brave woman's deed. A bus boycott was organized by the Blacks in retaliation for the arrest of Mrs. Parks and it was led by a then unknown young Baptist minister, Dr. Martin Luther King, Jr.

I sent another memorandum to Governor Adams about the racial strife in the South and asked permission to go to Alabama to talk with Black leaders about what they proposed to do in the future. I wanted the Administration to come to grips with this problem. I realized that it was fraught with political dangers and I was anxious for southern Blacks to know that they had not been abandoned by the Administration. Governor Adams sent for me. He said he appreciated my memorandum and had given it a great deal of thought, but that it would be politically and personally dangerous for me to be sent into the present situation. He obviously had FBI reports on the situation in Alabama. He said that communist influence was tremendous and he was certain that none of the responsible Blacks were aware of that fact.

The governor added that the matter was considered so serious that it would be discussed in a Cabinet meeting and in the Security Council and, if appropriate, J. Edgar Hoover of the FBI would go over the matter with the staff and the Attorney General would be asked to brief us on what was happening. He said he appreciated my position as a Black member of the President's staff, but I must not become deeply involved in the problem because I would become a target for reprisals that could be serious. He added that he would see to it that in the future I was completely briefed on what was happening, and that I could be certain that the President would never shirk his moral responsibility in this situation.

Just about this time another "manifesto" came out of Congress, castigating the Supreme Court for its anti-segregation decision as regards schools, and asserting that the decision went far beyond the Court's power to determine such an issue.

With all these fires raging in the forest of race relations in the South, it was inevitable that the President be queried about his attitude on civil rights at his next press conference. He was. In reply he appealed for level heads and again asked

Congress to consider the request in his State of the Union Message of two months ago to create a bipartisan commission to study this complex problem.

When asked by a reporter what he thought of the request of Harlem Representative Adam Clayton Powell to call together white and Black leaders in the South for a conference at the White House, the President indicated that he had rejected this idea. He felt action was needed, not discussion. He wanted a Congressional committee to do the reviewing, he said, because such a committee would have the power to subpoena and could get reluctant witnesses to talk and present evidence vital to any effective determination.

The hot summer of 1956 dragged on with Congress locked in debate on various civil rights recommendations. The administration continued its lukewarm stance on the question, and the introduction of civil rights legislation in the House came so late in the Congressional session that it smacked of a strategy to stymie passage since Congress wanted to adjourn for the political conventions. The Senate kept all civil rights bills confined within the Judiciary Committee until adjournment.

The Republican Party celebrating its one hundredth year held a convention in the Cow Palace in San Francisco on July 20, 1956. The results were preordained. Eisenhower was renominated by acclamation on July 22nd and Nixon was again selected as his running mate. I eagerly awaited the president's acceptance speech the next night. I had hoped that his speech challenging the party to greater effort in the future to secure the well-being of the American people would stress civil rights legislation. However, he gave the subject only a light brush in passing. He observed that "in all existing kinds of discrimination there is much to do."

The flight back to Washington was somber and foreboding. I could sense that this continued failure of the President to come to grips with civil rights and emerge as a staunch advocate of liberty and justice for all would lead to an Armageddon.

Eisenhower and Nixon won by a landslide in the November election. Interestingly enough, Eisenhower broke the Democratic stranglehold on the Black vote. In a departure from the Roosevelt New Deal era, Blacks gave the Republicans 47 percent of their votes. The fact of the return of a strong Black vote to the GOP induced some of the Administration stalwarts to make greater efforts in Congress to move civil rights legislation.

A month after the election Attorney General Brownell told Republican Congressional leaders that the president and the Department of Justice were going to resubmit the civil rights requests that had failed in Congress earlier. The President also indicated his intention to meet with party leaders and stress the importance of "moderate" civil rights legislation.

In the early part of 1957 the segregationists were on the rampage as they stopped Blacks from integrating public transportation and public places of accommodation. The buses in Montgomery carrying Blacks sitting forward, rather than in the rear according to custom, were fired upon daily. After a nighttime bombing of four Black churches in the city, all bus service was suspended. On February 14, dynamite destroyed the center of the Black district in Clinton, Tennessee. A KKK cross burned at the Marine Corps base in Camp Lejeune, North Carolina. It precipitated a race riot between Black and white servicemen.

In Americus, Georgia, Koinonia Farm, a communal group of Black and white people established more than fifteen years before, was dynamited and fired upon by whites in an effort to destroy the farm. The founder, Dr. Clarence Jordan, appealed to the President for help. The attorney general replied that the matter was not within federal jurisdiction.

My office was bedlam with telephone calls and protesting visitors. Sacks of mail came from bitter and angry people. They challenged my guts, manhood, and sense of decency. They demanded that I resign to show good faith. They denounced the President. It was ironic that just at this time the Administration decided to modify immigration requirements and to extend mutual security funds to provide for admission to the country of refugees from the Hungarian Revolution.

As I expected, the Blacks reacted angrily to the part the United States government played in welcoming the Hungarian refugees to this country. They resented the all-out effort of the Administration to see to it that the refugees were properly housed, clothed, fed, and given jobs commensurate with their skills. The Blacks pointed out that they were natives of this country and yet in most areas of the nation they were not properly housed, clothed, fed, or given jobs commensurate with their skills. Black social workers felt that Black clients in dire need of help often experienced great difficulty in having their needs met and in finding benevolent and sympathetic treatment. Yet, they said, in past weeks these same agencies had been bending over backward to meet the needs of Hungarian aliens.

I could not reason with my accusers on this emotional question. I knew that deep down Blacks were sympathetic to the plight of any benighted people. But how charitable can one expect Blacks to be when they so seldom experience any kind of public sympathy? The same problem faced me during World War II when there were racial separations in the armed forces. As a Black officer it was difficult to train and to give Black soldiers an incentive to fight for something most of them had never known at home. Their constant question was "Why were Black soldiers expected to go 3000 miles across the sea to fight and perhaps die for a way of life that they themselves had never experienced in their own country?"

On January 10, 1957, the President went to Capitol Hill to deliver his State of the Union address. I joined several staff members in guest seats in the rear of the House. The address was the shortest on record, and more philosophical in tone. The President stressed his hope that Congress would pass legislation increasing classrooms for all of the children of the country without regard to creed or color. He urged enactment of legislation to protect the civil rights of all citizens. Congress did not react enthusiastically. It appeared that Congress had no stomach for civil rights legislation.

A few days later I went up to the Hill to talk to the Vice President about my alarm over the situation in the South. Black homes and churches were being bombed and destroyed by disgruntled whites who were determined that the Supreme Court decisions on bus transportation and schooling would not be carried out. Naturally the response from Blacks was indignant and militant. Editorials in the Black press pointed out the similarities between the Blacks and the Hungarians, both of whom were victims of oppression, and stated that the Hungarians were getting a better break in their efforts to find freedom and succor.

The Vice President seemed earnestly concerned. His office was flooded with letters and telephone calls from distressed Blacks. They were urging him to come South and make a survey of their conditions as he did when he went to Hungary for the President. We both realized that he could not do this without having the Senate of the United States blow up in his face because of its continued intransigence on the subject of civil rights. What added to the din of Black discontent was the President's trip to the drought-stricken Southwest two days later. The President, wanting firsthand knowledge of the terrible destruction of valuable farm land in the Southwest, personally visited farms and farmers. His trip gave a real lift to the farmers and eased their grief and anguish.

A week before the President went to the Southwest, Martin Luther King, Jr. called a meeting in Atlanta of Black leaders from ten states to discuss the aftereffects of the recent bombings in Montgomery. The meeting resulted in the leaders sending an urgent request to the President to "come immediately" to a southern city to give "wise counsel" and to make a speech asking everybody to abide by the Supreme Court decision "as the law of the land." The President ignored their request and when questioned about it at a press conference, he replied that he had "a pretty good and sizeable agenda" on his desk every day and "as you know, I insist on going for a bit of recreation every once in a while. I do that because I think it's necessary to keep up with a state of fitness essential to this job." He added, "I don't know what another speech would do about the thing right now." Black frustration increased.

Through all these months it was harrowing for me to stand on a platform and make a speech or go before a college group or a Black group. I was ridiculed and censured because nothing was being done. What persuasive answer was there for these critics?

Chapter Seventeen

The Capital was preparing for Eisenhower's second inauguration and I became involved in some of the activities. I received an invitation from Doctor Edward L.R. Elson, pastor of the National Presbyterian Church which the President attended, to be present at a special preinauguration service to be held in the church on January 20th. I asked my fiancée, Catherine Boswell, to accompany me. We were asked to arrive at the church by 8:30 A.M.

The central portion of the large auditorium was roped off for members of the President's family, friends and staff. As Catherine and I entered, we were met by an usher who scrutinized our admittance cards for a long time. He appeared very upset and frantically called another usher who seemed to be in charge. It was apparent to us that this was an unexpected emergency. Apparently they had never anticipated that Blacks would attend the service. In a very cool manner we were ushered to a rear seat across from the roped-off section.

The guests were the great and powerful in American life. The service was an impressive one. All the favorite hymns of the President were sung and the choir was superb. At the close of the service I left Catherine standing just inside the door while I went to the cloakroom a few paces away for my coat. When I returned, she was flushed with anger. Two women members of the church had loudly discussed our presence. One commented caustically: "He must be a high government or foreign official, because if he were not, he would never dare enter our church."

I looked about me at the faces of colleagues, men with whom I worked every day. They ignored me. This often occurred when they were accompanied by their wives. Perhaps they felt they would have to introduce me in public. Naturally, their inability to treat me and my guest in a civil and courteous way left me angry.

The next day as I was about to leave my apartment for the Inaugural ceremony, my telephone rang. It was the President's secretary, Ann Whitman. She said that the President wanted to honor me by having me sit in his box after I had finished the parade route as a marshal. He included my fiancée in his invitation. The guests in the President's box included his family, his close personal friends of many years' standing, cabinet members and their wives and a handful of presidential assistants. The box was closely guarded by Secret Servicemen and the White House police. Even though I was well known to them, they acted as if they were uncertain that we were to be the President's guests. However, Ann Whiteman had fortified us with the coveted gold tickets. I escorted Catherine to the box and then went to take my place in the parade.

This was another "first." No other Black had served as a marshal of a division in the Inaugural parade.

Chapter Eighteen

During early February 1957, there was much excitement in the Black world over the birth of the new nation of Ghana, on the African Gold Coast. Ghana was to be established officially on March 6. The United States would be represented by the Vice President and an official delegation made up of members of Congress and other persons designated by the Secretary of State. Prime Minister Dr. Kwame Nkrumah had attended a Negro college in this country—Lincoln University—and had many friends here. Large private delegations planned to go to his inauguration, and great pressures were put on the White House and the State Department by prominent Blacks asking to be named to the official delegation from the United States. I was invited to be on the delegation.

On March 1, 1957, we landed in Rabat, Morocco to find a tremendous reception at the airport. A color guard had been drawn up and a Moroccan band played loud martial music.

The diplomatic corps was out in force and the Crown Prince of Morocco was there to extend the official welcome. It was a brilliant scene indeed! The Vice President went down the line to review the guard and then shook hands with the diplomatic corps. The area set aside for the ceremonies was gay with bunting and flags of all the nations and scores of gorgeous Persian rugs had been laid on the ground for VIPs to stand on. There were thousands of citizens in the background. Moroccan women have a queer throaty yell that they give whenever the Sultan or members of the royal family or visiting dignitaries pass by. It is a kind of warble. This is their manner of paying homage. It is all the more notable because the women are veiled, so you can't see how this sound is made.

After the ceremonies at the airport, we drove into Rabat. Thousands more lined the roadway and cheered as we passed. We could not help but be appalled by the scenes of overwhelming poverty and dirt and the obvious lack of sanitation.

The cavalcade was led by the Sultan's motorcycle corps, a kind of elite guard riding German motorcycles which were fast and light and were driven through the narrow streets at breakneck speed.

We entered Rabat, and drove toward the Imperial Palace, where we were to meet the Sultan. The scene was right out of *Arabian Nights*. The palace is a gigantic, sprawling structure covering many acres. Inside the huge white walls are superb gardens and tropical fruit trees. The roadway leading to the palace was lined with mounted guards on sleek Arabian horses. The royal band was playing Moroccan music outside the gate, and the mounted troops were brought to attention by French officers in command. We entered the gate and walked under a trellised arch into the building where the Sultan was waiting in the summer throne room. This was a gorgeous marble building with one side completely open facing the royal gardens. The wide interior was filled with fine fresco work and detailed carvings. The floors of the vast throne room were covered with Persian rugs piled a half-foot deep on top of each other.

The king was seated on the throne, and there were two seats on either side of him reserved for the Vice President and Mrs.

Nixon. After handshakes all around, the Sultan spoke through his interpreter. The Vice President responded, and this in turn was interpreted to the Sultan. The two men talked for a half hour and then we retired to take our places outside in a stand across from the palace where we were able to observe the King ride from the palace to the mosque to pray. Thousands of people lined the street from the palace to the temple to see this unique sight. The procession was led out of the palace gates by a band, followed by a squad of cavalry, and then, in a magnificently decorated carriage drawn by Arabian horses, came the Sultan. Beside and behind the carriage trekked the elders and the religious leaders of the court. Bringing up the rear, in a flashing brand-new Cadillac, was the Crown Prince. As the Sultan rode by the women gave their throaty yells and general ecstasy prevailed!

The Crown Prince seemed very pompous. He returned from the mosque in his Cadillac, came up to the stand where the Vice President was sitting, and proceeded to put on a very royal display. He was resplendent in a pristine white uniform with medals and other accoutrements, and seemed completely oblivious of the awed thousands who viewed him. It was at this point that the Nixons in typical American fashion left the stands to mingle with the people. The Vice President shook hands with scores of them, and Mrs. Nixon patted babies on the head and finally picked up a very dirty infant to cuddle. The crowd literally went crazy over this display of friendliness but it seemed to make the Crown Prince very uncomfortable. The Nixons were to do this same thing many times during their visit in Morocco and elsewhere, and newsmen later indicated that they knew both the Sultan and the Crown Prince would be glad when we left. Royalty does *not* mingle with peasants, and this display of American democracy at work might very well put queer ideas into the people's heads.

That night the Prime Minister held a lavish reception and dinner for us at the Guest House. It was the kind of dinner that would be repeated many times on this trip: native dishes washed down with appropriate wines and two or three hour meals accompanied by positive exhaustion!

We left for Casablanca by car the next morning in a fast and furious motorcade, our way cleared by the elite motorcycle guard which went at lightning speed down the twisting, turning cement roads. Police estimated that more than 200,000 delirious cheering people took part in the welcoming demonstration in Casablanca. They crowded every rooftop, tree, telegraph pole, and square inch of the city to get a glimpse of Mr. Nixon. The local police and the Secret Service accompanying us were very nervous. The Vice President's car was slowed to a halt as the people scrambled around it to shake his hand or to cheer him, and at several points he got out of the car to circulate and greet them.

After a tour of the city, we went to a luncheon given by the businessmen of Casablanca at the city hall. It was easy to understand why business shuts down for four hours in the middle of the day. We were the victims of an eight-course luncheon in the searing heat, and it was almost unbearable. Here again we were overwhelmed with choice native dishes and none of us was in the mood to tackle the huge meal. Particularly discouraging was a whole pigeon laden with sauces and creams. Since we were on a goodwill tour, it was not possible to ignore this hospitality, but it was almost more than my stomach could stand.

In Accra the first pleasant surprise to meet us was the beautiful and modern hotel that the Ghana Government had erected for the delegates and visitors to the Independence Celebration. The maitre d'hotel was German, but the waiters and other functionaries were natives. The manager told us that six weeks before our arrival the African employees had never seen a hotel, been inside of one, or had any knowledge of any of their tasks. He and his wife and a small staff had organized them so that they could function the day the hotel opened—about a week before we arrived. There were some snarls, of course, and it was difficult at times to make the hotel personnel understand what we wanted. We discovered that an African never says, "I do not understand." He may make a dozen tries to come up with what you want, but in his efforts he is always smiling and shaking his head with a vigorous nod to show that he understands!

The next day I went with the Vice President to meet Prime

Minister Nkrumah at Government House at 7:00 A.M. I had not expected the government buildings to be so large or so modern. A prominent area of Accra had been staked out for the various ministry buildings and in the center of these modern structures was Government House, a magnificent building of marble and native stone.

Even at this early hour in the morning, the custom of serving all guests with glasses of champagne was being observed. All members of the diplomatic corps were present as were the official delegates from various countries around the world. Prime Minister Nkrumah was obviously glad to see the Vice President, who, upon being presented, immediately introduced me as his assistant. The Prime Minister expressed great delight at my presence and as soon as he could get away from his other guests he led me into a corner and immediately launched into a discussion of the significance of the occasion.

Nkrumah was an inspiring man, humble, and a little bewildered about what had happened so suddenly in his country—but impressed with his great responsibility to make this new endeavor work. He congratulated me upon my position on the President's staff and agreed that we both had something in common, since we were both pioneering in difficult fields. He urged me to come back to talk again, and said that after six months he hoped to be able to travel and looked forward to coming to the United States at an early date. We promised to keep in touch.

That afternoon we went out to the enormous athletic stadium, where a celebration was being held. It was one of the largest gatherings I had ever seen. The stadium was lined with soldiers, both cavalry and footmen, and with representatives from the scores of tribes in the country who had come to Accra for the celebration. We were treated to a colorful review by the troops and by tribal dances from the many tribes represented.

At the appropriate moment in the ceremony there was a flurry of trumpets, the movement of cavalry units through the gate, and in a long black Rolls-Royce—with footmen and outriders—Her Royal Highness the Duchess of Kent, representing Great Britain, made her entrance into the stadium.

The scene resembled a Coronation Parade in London, when the newly crowned monarch rides from the palace to the cathedral for the ceremony. It was indeed an inspiring sight, and the thousands of people in the stadium cheered, screamed, and shouted as the Duchess, who is very regal looking, vivacious and attractive, waved from the royal limousine. She entered the stands and took her place in the Royal Box with the Prime Minister, who had walked down to meet her.

The first thing on the program the following day, March 5, was a convocation at the University College. I was pleasantly surprised by the physical appearance of the college which is located on a hill several miles outside of Accra. The buildings are white stone and stucco, and very attractive. The academic procession was indeed impressive, with the regalia of the officials in the line of march and the multi-colored hoods of professors from various colleges in England and Europe. The college staff was predominantly white and it appeared that most of the professors had been recruited from countries abroad. The Vice President, Mrs. Nixon, and I joined the crowd pouring into the auditorium and we had some difficulty finding seats until we were rescued by an official usher. We were in the center of the hall, and it was stiflingly hot. We all hoped that the ceremony would not be long.

The candidates for graduation were presented to the Duchess of Kent, and her response, in the form of a short address, brought greetings from Her Majesty the Queen, and noted that it was a glorious day both for the mother country and for the young men and women being graduated there.

On our way out we ran into the Reverend and Mrs. Martin Luther King, Jr. of Birmingham, Alabama who had come for the celebration. This was a coincidence. Dr. King had been trying to see the Vice President for many months back in the States, and here—several thousand miles away—the two men meet face to face. The Vice President invited King to call upon him during his next visit to Washington. This meeting made headlines in the Black press, because King was the current hero in Black America, having successfully led the bus boycott in Montgomery, Alabama. I was grateful for the Vice President's ease in handling the situation. Anything less tactful could have made derogatory headlines for the Republicans in the Black press back home.

We made a visit to a native village high up in the hills. The experience was terrific. The paramount chief, the subchiefs, and the whole village turned out to greet us. It was like the scenes of villages in the heart of Africa that one sees in the movies. We were taken inside the compound and given seats of honor under huge colored umbrellas. The natives then did their welcoming dance. The Vice President spoke to the people of the village, and his words were interpreted to them in their native tongue. They were so overjoyed by the friendliness of the group that even the paramount chief danced to honor the Vice President! This was unprecedented. Paramount chiefs maintain all the dignity and regal bearing of any ruler of state, and to see this kingly man leave his throne, push aside his attendants, and begin one of the delirious African dances, was really something to behold.

About nine at night, I got into a white dinner jacket and accompanied the Vice President to the out-of-door reception given by the Speaker of the House on the spacious grounds of Accra's Parliament House. They were crowded with people. Colored lights placed in the flower beds added a glow to the crowds of dignitaries from all over the world. It was a beautiful sight. The Vice President presented the Speaker with a gavel made from the old wood from the White House.

At midnight Ghana became a nation. The Union Jack was hauled down from the Parliament House staff at the stroke of twelve, and the red, yellow, and green national flag of the new nation was raised in its place. "At long last," Kwame Nkrumah shouted to a crowd of 12,000 rapt Africans, "the battle has ended; Ghana, our beloved country, is free forever. Let us pause for one minute to give thanks to Almighty God." For sixty seconds the crowd stood silent. Then a mighty roar shook the air: "Ghana is free!" I was awakened later by the blowing of taps which marked the end of colonialism in Ghana and the beginning of a new independence. I could hear the thousands of cheering voices, and it was a strange and stimulating feeling to lie there in the darkness and realize the significance of this moment in the history of humanity.

Chapter Nineteen

In Liberia there was a formal dinner at the American Embassy given by Vice President Nixon for President William V.S. Tubman. The embassy is beautifully located on a cliff overlooking the ocean and makes an imposing picture for miles around.

On March 10 we landed at Entebbe, Uganda around ten o'clock in the morning. It was a scenic flight, coming into this lush little area right on Lake Victoria, the third largest and one of the most beautiful lakes in the world. There was the usual band playing martial music and a contingent of Black ceremonial troops commanded by British officers.

The Hotel Victoria where I was lodged was a fascinating place. It was loaded with Black houseboys and waiters who moved about the hotel barefooted, some in long white gowns with green sashes and red fezzes—others in less stylish garments which looked like brown denim rompers. The barefooted waiters would slog around the banquet and dining halls and houseboys polished the hardwood floors by standing on rags in their bare feet and going around in circles to rub the polish into the wood. They spoke in several dialects, so it was difficult to communicate. The hotel was run by the English and run very well.

In the evening a white-tie dinner was given by the Governor General and Lady Crawford at Government House—a typical spit-and-polish affair. The Oxford diction was a yard thick, and all the guests were highly educated and interesting people. A Black police band in handsome uniforms played good dinner music. It was one of the most interesting evenings of the trip. The food and drink were good—the conversation stimulating. Entebbe is a garden spot of Africa and one of the most beautiful places I have ever seen. The British had done their usual job of making themselves comfortable and developing a splendid civilization in this unique area of the Dark Continent. Despite my extreme dislike for colonialism and everything it denotes, I could not deny that the British really benefit any place into which they move. They provided all the preliminary essentials such as good roads, fine water systems, functional hotels, and the ever-present golf courses.

We left Entebbe on March 11 at 1:00 P.M. for a four-hour flight to Addis Ababa, Ethiopia. On the plane we changed from street clothes to cutaways, striped trousers, and high hats, for the official arrival in the Ethiopian capital. We landed at five and were met by the Crown Prince, heir apparent to the throne, and other high Ethiopian officials. We piled into smart European cars and went directly from the airport to the Jubilee Palace, home of the Crown Prince, where the Nixons were to stay. The rest of us were quartered at the Ghion Hotel, an excellent hotel with all modern appointments, across from the palace.

We drove to the Imperial Palace for an audience with his Imperial Majesty, Haile Selassie. The ride to the palace was fascinating. There were thousands of poor Ethiopians outside the huge gates, watching our procession enter. It was a sight that cried out the inequities of absolute monarchy. We proceeded up the long, winding drive to the top of the hill where the palace sprawls over several acres. There were soldiers guarding every inch of the drive, and the stone steps at the entrance leading up to the palace were crowded with dozens of top brass and functionaries. We were escorted through a long hall to the door of the throne room. When this door was opened, we looked into fairyland. The King and Queen were on throne chairs in the gorgeous setting of a block-long room. The floors were smothered in costly rugs and brocaded draperies hung to the floor from windows more than thirty feet high. All about were fabulous treasures. Man-sized vases and urns stood in corners all over the room and golden treasures were in evidence at every turn.

The King and Queen were flanked by three royal highnesses and a niece. The aide-de-camp introduced the Vice President and Mrs. Nixon to His Royal Majesty, and after a brief chat, the Vice President introduced his staff. We all made low bows from the waist and shook hands. The King gave me a double handshake and whispered in perfect English, "I am glad to see you." This was startling to me, because in the United States the word was that Ethiopia was not kindly disposed toward American Blacks and not until very recently were they acceptable in Ethiopia in any capacity.

The legend is that Ethiopians do not want to be identified with the lowly plight of American Blacks. The Ethiopian is brown in color but his features are the chiseled ones of the Arab or Hamitic race. But my reception was warm and sincere and I had a feeling that these scores of impeccably clothed and highly educated court functionaries were not only surprised but rather proud to see a brown man in the Vice President's entourage.

I could look out of my hotel window and still see the thousands of people who had lined the streets to view us as we came from the airport to the palace. They were still standing in the cold rain, and they looked wet, bedraggled and defeated. They shuffled about in colorful dress and costume, in streets that were clogged with two-wheeled carts pulled by donkeys or spavined horses.

Other than the large cars in the Emperor's fleet, most of the cars we saw in Addis Ababa were small foreign models that one would see in the hilly country of Europe. There was utter chaos in the streets of Addis Ababa. Traffic went in all four directions at the same time without pattern or police to direct it. It was worth one's life to drive, ride, or walk in this confusion. There was the constant honking of horns, braying of donkeys, and shouting of pedestrians—utter bedlam.

We were astonished by the backward appearance of the country. Ethiopia, high up in the mountains, was inaccessible to most of the world until the invention of the airplane. There is much poverty and illiteracy and few of the ordinary comforts of life. The contrast of the pageantry and color of the royal family with the poverty of the great mass of people was striking. I wondered whether democracy could thrive and grow in a country that has lived like this for centuries. The only thing these people had ever known was worship of the Emperor. Perhaps more privileges of citizenship could be granted but I doubted very much if the average American idea of democracy could be transplanted easily in this ancient country.

The formal state dinner was at the imperial palace. Upon arrival, the Vice President's party was escorted to the throne room to await a summons to the upstairs reception room where the Emperor and the Queen would receive the guests. The diplomatic corps had been assembled in another room. Soon we were escorted up a beautiful winding stairway to the second floor and entered a gigantic room in which the Emperor and Queen were standing on a royal rug. The Emperor was resplendent in formal dress uniform, and his imperial staff, bemedaled and standing stiffly at attention, formed a dramatic background. The Vice President and Mrs. Nixon joined the Emperor and Queen, and the rest of us stood just beside the Emperor's staff. After this maneuver, the royal announcer went to a door, pulled back a heavily brocaded curtain, and beckoned the diplomatic corps to the door. He announced the name of the ambassadors and their wives. Each couple walked forward ten steps; the women curtsied and the men bowed. They would go another ten steps and do the same thing, finally reaching the royal rug. Again they would curtsy and bow, shaking hands with both the Emperor and the

Queen, and then move slowly backward into the royal dining room to find their places at a table.

Some of the women's dresses were so long and close-fitting that when they went to curtsy, they almost fell on their faces. Those were tense moments for me as I stood there watching this endless line of foreign representatives go through this ritual, hoping each time that they would be able to get up to the royal rug and away without disaster. I was interested in the Russian ambassador and his wife. They walked in, stolid and unsmiling, but went through the ritual like everyone else.

After this procession of ninety or more people, Mrs. Nixon took the Emperor's arm, and the Queen the Vice President's and behind them we entered the royal dining room. The dining room was at least two New York City blocks long, gorgeously decorated, and the floors covered with rugs well piled at least six inches deep. The table, placed in the center of the room, ran the entire length of the hall, seating 125 people. The room was ablaze with light from gold candelabra, gold vases filled with every conceivable kind of flower, and the gleaming reflections from the gold table service. Everything in the room was gold. Even the chairs and table had the royal crest emblazoned in gold.

There were scores of waiters and assistants. The waiters wore white gloves, green velvet cutaways, red knee breeches, white stockings, and black patent leather slippers with silver buckles. The head butler wore the customary formal dress of white tie, while his assistants wore blue jackets with gold epaulets on their shoulder and red trousers. Somewhere in the courtyard a string orchestra played softly during the meal. The menu was written in both Amharic and French.

I sat between two medal-laden Cabinet members. They spoke Amharic, Italian, Spanish, and French. With my limited French we exchanged a few pleasantries, but state dinners were a strain for me in any foreign country because of the language difficulties. At an appropriate moment champagne glasses were raised by the Emperor to toast the Vice President and the President of the United States. The Vice President returned the toast. I downed the native foods with great difficulty. Each time a white-gloved hand would offer me a dish of some weird concoction, I would have to copy the actions of my tablemates and take whatever portion they took. I did not think I was going to make it.

There was the usual official procession to the airport in a cavalcade made up of members of the royal household and various Ethiopian dignitaries. By nine o'clock on March 13, we were en route to Khartoum, Sudan. After a flight of several hours we landed in Sudan without incident. The Sudanese are a reserved people and their welcoming demonstration was less noisy and uninhibited. They had enjoyed freedom for only a year and they were wearing it with dignity and a deep sense of responsibility.

We were given lavish quarters in a great palace which had been headquarters for English governors for many years. It was an incredible mansion, overlooking the Nile, and apparently had also been used as a barracks to house both English and native troops during the long period of occupation. Shortly after our arrival we began round after round of teas with the chiefs of small communities in the area. A huge one, staged that afternoon on the grounds of the palace where we were staying, was a fantastic sight. We mingled with thousands of Sudanese in colorful dress and met powerful chieftains from the many tribes who had come to pay their respects to the Vice President of the United States.

We were particularly awed by our first formal meal in the palace as guests of the Prime Minister. The principal course was fish which was placed on the table in its original size of a small whale. It had been baked whole, and each guest was permitted to cut his or her own piece. We were given native tools to do this: the knife was the size of a sword and the utensil used to place the fish on one's plate was the size of a small kitchen shovel. The fish was delicious but it had lots of bones which made precarious eating for unskilled Americans. However, the atmosphere was friendly and we were able to glimpse the intelligence of this young nation's top leaders.

On March 14, 1957, we were airborne early enroute to Tripoli, Libya. The stewards aboard the plane had been thoughtful enough to prepare coffee, fruit juice, and toast, and a few minutes after we were aloft we were enjoying this light

American breakfast. We crossed the great Sahara Desert again and it was an awesome sight as we looked down from 12,000 feet to see nothing but endless miles of sand. You couldn't help wondering what it would be like to land in this eternal waste of sand.

We were flying blithely along, chatting about our hours in Khartoum, when all of a sudden one of the starboard motors backfired and then quit completely. We all looked at each other, not so much in fright, but with stunned surprise! We could feel the plane lose a bit of altitude and were conscious of the pilot's efforts to restart the motor. Even before the pilot told us, we were aware of the fact that we were circling to start a crippled flight back to Khartoum. As soon as we had made the circle, the pilot requested Mr. Nixon to come forward right away. After a few minutes, he returned to tell us that possibly we could have limped into Tripoli on three motors but the pilot would rather not take this chance. We were to return to Khartoum for repairs. The pilot had wired ahead to the airfield to inform the Prime Minister that we were returning.

Despite this assurance from the pilot and the Vice President, we put two anxious hours on this return flight. There were still many harrowing miles ahead of us before we would reach home and we began to wonder whether we should risk crossing the Atlantic in this plane, despite the fact that it was one of the most plush jobs in the Air Force. Since it was a personal plane of Admiral Radford, Chairman of the Joint Chiefs of Staff, there was every reason to believe that it would be completely safe and reliable.

A tremendous celebration awaited us in Tripoli and the newsmen, who had left an hour ahead to record our arrival, had a great story in our failure to arrive on time. It was possible that they would send the story via cable and wireless, which could alarm our families and friends at home.

We made the trip back to Khartoum safely. The Prime Minister came to take the Vice President and Mrs. Nixon back to the palace and the rest of us decided to buy souvenirs for friends in the small shops surrounding the airport.

We waited around for more than four hours, but the plane

from Tripoli arrived about noon, and its mechanics went right to work. Also arriving from another African base was a "rescue plane" which would follow us for the rest of our trip. On our second try we reached Tripoli without incident, arriving over the city as darkness fell. It was beautiful to come into that ancient city just as lights were being turned on in the little dwellings below and we zoomed down onto the runway of the air base located off the seaport that was once an operating area for pirates. The United States had built a massive installation in Tripoli, and it was a genuine oasis in that faraway section of the world.

After a typical American celebration we were hustled off to a barracks that had been provided for our use. The Nixons were given quarters at the home of the commanding general. Our first concern was getting laundry done. The special services officer of the base had cleared the decks so that all facilities were at our disposal and our laundry and cleaning were collected as soon as we were able to get them together. We were not so happy four hours later when our laundry was returned clean but with nearly all the buttons shorn from the shirts. We were immediately issued GI sewing kits by the commanding officer. We went to work and were soon ready to enjoy our short stay in that historic seaport town.

The next morning we were shown several places of interest. The signs of great poverty and primitive living were overpowering. Many of the local people were in rags and it was obvious that their efforts to make a life in this impoverished area were almost futile. Their life and dwellings contrast with Tripoli's government buildings which are modern and efficient. We found the various city officials deeply concerned about their responsibilities to help people secure a better way of life.

We had traveled many thousands of miles in Africa, across jungles and deserts, but we did not see our first camel until we reached Tripoli. It was not plodding across some wide expanse of desert, but was being used as a beast of burden by a peddler hawking his wares on the hot asphalt streets.

While we were sight-seeing, I was startled when a young woman ran out of the crowd shouting my name. She waved for the driver to stop. When he did, she stuck her head in the car and I recognized her as a former secretary at the Republican National Committee. She had been spending the last year in Tripoli with her father who was there on a mission for the State Department. This was a very pleasant surprise. Later that day she brought her mother and father to our quarters at the air base to have tea. I had a similar happy meeting with a former Army buddy who had remained in the service and was now a major and a jet pilot attached to one of the outfits at the Tripoli air base.

It was comforting to us to see and appreciate the need for these great air bases in various sections of the world. They are vital for our national security, and are equipped to do an effective job whenever they are called upon. All day and all night—as long as we remained at this base—jet squadrons were taking off for or returning from some important mission. The Air Force has done an excellent job in trying to give its personnel on these far-off bases most of the comforts and a few of the luxuries of home.

The highlight of the visit to Rome during our return trip was our personal audience with Pope Pius XII. I believe that this must be a stirring moment in any human's life no matter what one's religion or creed when he comes into the presence of the one who is the symbol of one of the world's great religions. Certainly I, a Protestant, was visibly moved.

The Vatican is a tiny self-contained city. One is conscious of being in one of earth's most historic communities as soon as one enters the gates. The Vatican has all the tradition, pomp, and ceremony of past centuries and the Swiss guards, with their extraordinary uniforms and ancient weapons, are like soldiers from a fantastic fairytale.

We were given the red carpet treatment, and each of us in the official party was offered the privilege of shaking hands with the Pope and saying a few words to him. We were told that, since he was a very delicate man, we were to take his hand lightly and shake it gently. Since he could not speak loudly, we were advised to keep as quiet as possible and not take more than a few minutes with him, so as not to tax his strength.

Mrs. Nixon had purchased a special outfit for the occasion,

a floor-length black gown and a gorgeous black lace mantilla. The Vice President's personal secretary, Rose Mary Woods, was similarly dressed. The men wore morning clothes or dark blue suits.

When we entered the Pope's study, he was standing to greet us and we were all surprised when he gave each of us a firm, warm handshake, saying how glad he was to see us. He read greetings from a typewritten page, expressing his gratitude for our visit and his deep respect for President Eisenhower, Mr. Nixon, and the American people in general. Then he presented each of us with a beautiful silver medal embossed with his picture—commemorating the eighteenth year of his reign—and raised his slim, patrician hands to give us his blessing and benediction.

We left Rome early for Tunisia on March 18. Tunisia was a tiny, poverty-stricken nation on the Mediterranean shore of North Africa. Its population was half that of New York City yet it was playing an important role in Arab and world affairs. Free of France which ruled it until the previous year, Tunisia had come to represent a nation friendly to the West.

We were met at the airport with the usual courtesies from the dignitaries of the country, led by Prime Minister Habib Bourguiba. Our motorcade left immediately for the palace of the Bey of Tunis, the last of the fabulous monarchs of that area. The bey had become a mere symbol of past glories, since Tunisia was well on its way toward eliminating all royal prerogatives and becoming a practicing democracy. Mr. Bourguiba appeared to be "the strong man" and our information indicated that the bey would probably be exiled in the very near future and Bourguiba would become the first president of the country.

We were received in the bey's palace with all the pomp and ceremony expected of a king, and again, as in Morocco, this was like a glimpse into an ancient storybook. This is a land of fezzes and veiled women and Western dress looked rather odd. The usual welcoming speeches were made and the usual expressions of friendship tendered. The bey gave the Vice President a jeweled watch to be presented to President Eisenhower. We were told that it had cost several thousand dollars and had been made especially for the President.

After our palace visit, we were taken to our guest house—a fabulous palace overlooking the Mediterranean. The surroundings, appointments, and furnishings made any we had seen in other sections of the world appear drab. It was certainly on a par with the royal domain of Haile Selassie. It was built entirely of marble with huge winding staircases and the floors were covered with fabulously valuable Oriental rugs. Our bedrooms were the size of small ballrooms and each bed could have held four people. There were two or three attendants for each of us and their garb was wonderful. They wore red fezzes, white mess jackets, red pantaloons, and odd shoes that turned up at the toes. They moved swiftly and softly about the house and no matter where one might be in the castle, one was always in the vicinity, ready to do one's bidding. I could easily understand why so many of history's kings and members of royalty suffered and died from tuberculosis. Despite the 100° heat outside, these palaces are always cold and dank. After being in them for an hour or so, it is good to get out in the heat and get warm.

Every effort was made to give us all the luxuries of home. A bar where every conceivable kind of American drink was available was set up in a small downstairs room. The native bartenders could not understand us and we had great fun trying to get them to serve us the drinks we wanted. Soon we became very proficient in gestures and self-service.

We were located in Tunis, the capital city, and during our visit the country was at the height of celebrating the first year of its freedom. There were endless parades which kept traffic in a continuous snarl, and the people were in a jubilant and festive mood.

I begged off from the formal dinner given for us because there were certain to be more of the bizarre dishes that I had fallen victim to in Morocco and Ethiopia. I spent my first free evening sitting around the palace and socializing with some of the younger members of the American Embassy staff. Later I went to the home of the second secretary of the embassy and it was pleasant to find that many members of the American colony had charming homes on the edge of this cliff overlooking the Mediterranean. It was a beautiful location and they were able to run out of their homes down to the water's edge for swimming or boating.

One enjoys being the guest of Americans in far-off countries because they make such a fuss over you; you are fresh from America and have the latest news. Americans living abroad are eager to be brought up to date on what is happening back home. I am certain that most persons serving our embassies make a real effort to be friendly with local people and to cultivate neighborly relationships with foreigners, but it is understandable that they have a tendency to form closely knit groups of their own. This naturally has its drawbacks. It leads the officials of the host country to believe that Americans are inherent snobs and that they feel superior to the local citizens. I don't feel that these accusations are entirely true but I do think that we should make greater efforts to become friendly with the citizens of the countries where we serve.

Once my identity was established, I had a wonderful time in Tunis. People in this part of the world seldom see American Blacks, and certainly not one who has a position of any consequence in the United States Government. I also believe that American Blacks have the ability to make friends with foreigners, if for no other reason than the fact that they know what it means to be discriminated against. I found them eager and anxious to help me at every turn and the palace staff seemed particularly pleased to have me as a guest.

My first night in these strange surroundings resulted in fitful slumber. My room opened out on a beautiful court and with the windows wide open, a desert moon shone brightly into the room. In the stillness of the desert one can hear all the weird sounds of the night. The only difficulty about open windows in this area of the world is that if they are not screened the room becomes full of countless strange bugs and insects.

I awoke with a start about 6:30 the next morning, conscious that someone was in my room. The sun was streaming in brightly, and when I raised myself to a sitting position, I was startled by the sight of four red-fezzed gentlemen in pantaloons, standing by my bed, watching me. I had no idea what this strange scene meant and I had difficulty orienting myself.

They were there merely to help. In Tunis, it is customary for one's personal servants to be present at the bedside in the morning when one awakens. One of them held a tray with a silver coffeepot and service ready to pour me a piping hot cup. Another was holding a gold tray laden with tropical fruits. The other two carried bath towels, soap, and a huge terry-cloth robe for me to wrap myself in when emerging from the ancient bath. They had no intention of deserting me, despite my protestations, and they stayed with me until I was completely dressed and ready to go downstairs for breakfast.

During the day, members of the embassy staff who served as our guides drove us several miles outside Tunis to view the ruins of a once glorious city. We later visited a very beautiful cemetery on a cliff overlooking the Mediterranean where many of the heroic American soldiers who lost their lives in World War II are buried.

One of the most unique experiences of our visit was our trip to the Souks, the native area where hundreds of little shops are located. It is in the oldest section of the city, and is a melange of dirt, confusion, and poverty. The visit to the Souks was made doubly dangerous by the wild and drunken celebrants. They were tossing exploding firecrackers in all directions and it was a wonder that many people were not injured. This caused Mrs. Nixon to cut short her shopping tour in this area, and it was with some trepidation that the male members of our group remained to try to find a few bargains in copper trays, scatter rugs, or leather goods. We were getting near the end of our trip and were all looking for gifts to take home. We had three exciting and enjoyable days in this small desert country, but were happy when our planes pointed toward home, with our first stop in the Azores.

Our trip to the Azores was uneventful, but it is an odd experience to be on a plane that is trying to pick out a small spit of land in the midst of a vast ocean. The plane's searchlights danced across the water, looking for familiar landmarks, and the uninitiated passenger was only aware of the dark water below. One sits at a window and strains his eyes to see exactly why the pilot is coming down to land where there apparently is no land at all. Not until one feels the familiar bump of the plane wheels on the runway is any sense of security assured.

The press plane had arrived a half hour ahead of us, and the correspondents were already busy stuffing handfuls of quarters into the dozen or more slot machines in the club. Others were trying to make last-minute purchases of a few bottles of whiskey which sold for two or three dollars less than in the States. Even though we were on special planes, we were rigidly held to the rules and regulations governing customs, and each of us was permitted to take back only three bottles of liquor.

The commanding officer and the ranking officials of the big air base at the Azores were present to greet us, despite the fact that it was 1:30 A.M. The Nixons were carried off to the commandant's home for breakfast and the rest of us went to the officer's club. The huge planes were refueled and we were ready to take off again in about an hour and a half. Weather reports indicated that we might find severe head winds, slowing our homeward progress, so the planes were turned toward Newfoundland, rather than Bermuda, since the weather reports in that area seemed better.

All I had to do was lie in my bunk and wait for dawn. It was thrilling to sight the frozen wasteland of Newfoundland in the early light. We did not stop for refueling, but continued toward Washington. As soon as land was sighted, all of us seemed to feel much better. It was a jubilant, happy group that got ready for breakfast as our plane streaked across the coast of Maine. We reached the airport at Washington about noon, and were given a heartwarming reception. We all posed for a final picture coming down the ramp and it was with real regret that we said goodbye after four thrilling weeks together in far-off sections of the world.

I returned from Africa aware of a new dimension in my desire to be of assistance in helping my Black brothers and sisters at home and abroad arise from the depths of deprivation, discrimination, and isolation. Visiting the newly emerging countries in Africa whetted my appetite to forge an awareness of the inter-related problems and solutions of the color question throughout the world. My talks with Nkrumah of

Ghana, Azewei of Nigeria, and Tubman of Liberia reaffirmed my belief that the same philosophy of "white superiority and supremacy" that kept Black Africa in subjection and ignorance for centuries was the same philosophy that had kept American Blacks handcuffed to slavery and its aftermath for 300 years. There was a kinship here of African and American Black identity and if carefully nurtured and developed it could lead to world revolt against human injustice and denial.

The African leaders had leveled with me and revealed their intense desire to develop a solidarity with American Blacks in the cause of freedom and recognition. They felt that American Blacks must press harder for their rights and be ready to die for them; and that American Black leaders must learn not to bargain for and accept the appearance for the substance! I could understand the African's reluctance at first to ask for Black American ambassadors. They felt the Blacks, still second-class citizens in their own country, would not have the leverage in high places in the United States to benefit the African country to which they might be accredited. I promised to keep in touch with these leaders, and back at home, I would be available to their ambassadors in the United States for consultation and advice.

A few weeks after my return from the trip, I was asked to speak at a White House staff meeting on my experiences and findings. In a brief talk I gave the highlights and the pleas from the African leaders for understanding. But what astonished the staff most—and also produced the most laughter—was my answer to the question: "What impressed you most of all in the countries visited?"

I said, ". . . for the first time in my life, I was a member of the *majority*, and it was a damn nice feeling . . ."

Chapter Twenty

During the spring of 1957, Blacks were still devising methods to make the administration move on civil rights. A. Philip Randolph in 1941 had threatened a "march on Washington" with thousands of marchers, to make President Roosevelt grant a Federal Employment Personnel Commission for federal employees. There were plans to resurrect such a plan now in 1957. At the Southern Christian Leadership Conference meeting in New Orleans in February, Dr. King issued a warning that continued presidential stubbornness would cause thousands of whites and Blacks to march to Washington. Out of this determination for a showdown in Washington, a "Prayer Pilgrimage for Freedom" was planned for May 17, the third anniversary of the Supreme Court's school desegregation decision. This pilgrimage was to be a "spiritual" rather than a "political" demonstration. The ministers involved in the planning hoped such a designation would arouse the nation's conscience and nudge the President and the Congress into some kind of action.

On May 17, the Prayer Pilgrimage brought 20,000 Blacks from all over the United States to Washington. The ceremony went off without any untoward incidents. But, frankly, the effect of the pilgrimage was a zero as far as the Administration was concerned. It received little press coverage, and a "ho-hum" attitude prevailed in official Washington. Using hindsight, the only thing the march did was to foreshadow the gigantic and earth-shaking Civil Rights march in 1963.

Through the hot summer months of July and August, we wrestled with the problem of trying to get the President to accede to the wishes of Martin King, Roy Wilkins, and A. Philip Randolph and admonish the South on its outright flaunting of the Supreme Court's edict on schools. We discussed ad nauseam the feasibility of a meeting of the President and American Black leaders to review the question of civil rights legislation. There was a unanimous, continuous rejection of this by other presidential advisors. The atmosphere in the nation was so bad on this problem that Mrs. Ogden Reid, publisher of the *New York Herald Tribune*, told Sherman Adams that the majority of Blacks felt that the President had let them down on the matter of civil rights. She felt something had to be done immediately to allay this feeling. Adams asked me how I felt about this. I assured him that Mrs. Reid was right and that the time was now to take some positive steps. I suggested that the President, without further delay, meet with Dr. King and his committee. Adams agreed but said we would have to hold off until Congress had voted the President's budget up or down. At the moment the Congress was running wild pruning the budget and this activity created a tense and unhappy White House. The President was not in a good mood for any civil rights maneuvering.

However, A. Philip Randolph kept bombarding the White House with requests for a meeting with the President. His third had just been received and this time he asked to bring sixteen other persons with him. Max threw up trial balloons on this matter with presidential assistants, and they were not enthusiastic. They argued that sixteen was too many, and that this was not a strategic time to hold such a meeting when the Civil Rights Bill was being cuffed around in Congress. The bill had already passed the House and the southern members of the Senate were now engaged in delaying tactics to keep it bottled up until Congress adjourned. Any visit with the President by Black leaders could be interpreted by the Senators as pressure to make them act. I was also told that if this request was honored, the White House would have to accede to requests from southern governors, southern attorneys general, Americans of Italian and Greek descent who wanted to talk about immigration, Jewish people concerned about Israel, and Hungarians or Lithuanians who wanted independence.

During those "dog days" of 1957 in nearly unbearable heat, I was engaging in my annual exercise of trying to find better living quarters. The daily papers were full of attractive offers of houses or apartments to rent, but none was available to me, because of my color. I despaired of driving by and seeing the horrible rat holes and dilapidated houses that were advertised "For Colored" in the newspapers. God! This has always been one of our nightmares in almost any community in the country. We cannot, without struggling and fighting, find a decent place to live!

Late in August, the first Civil Rights Act since Reconstruction passed through a reluctant Congress. It was a pitiful, watered down version of the original bill emasculated by amendments added by southern Senators. Some Black leaders, including certain executives of the NAACP, urged support of the watered down version, on the theory that half a loaf is better than no bread at all. I was shocked. For more than forty years the NAACP had been uncompromising in its attitude that human rights were not to be dealt out piecemeal to American citizens, nor should there be legislation indicating willingness on the part of the government to insure and protect *only certain rights*. However, the Afro-American newspaper came out supporting the half-loaf theory. The President signed it.

The Civil Rights Act of 1957 established a Civil Rights Division in the Justice Department and an independent Commission on Civil Rights with subpoena powers.

Chapter Twenty-one

The first ten days of September, 1957 were tragic ones in which the press, the radio, and television depicted the bitter, bloody struggle going on in Arkansas, Alabama, and Tennessee, as Blacks made efforts to enroll in white schools in accordance with the Supreme Court decision of 1954. Little Rock particularly took the spotlight as the governor determined that no matter what federal courts decreed, Arkansas would ignore and defy federal authority.

Little Rock's Central High School was to be integrated in September following the orders of a federal district court. Both the school board and the mayor approved the plan and nine Black students were to be admitted without incident. However, Governor Orval Faubus brazenly boasted that his refusal to go along with the plans would "divide this state and eventually the nation." Faubus, a wily political figure, was trying to exploit this vexatious problem for his own gain.

When the White Citizens Council campaigned against the desegregation plan, Faubus joined the effort. The day before school opened, Faubus predicted violence if the plan went into effect, so he called out the Arkansas National Guard to keep the Black students from entering Central High School.

President Eisenhower in July had emphasized the fact that he did not want to use federal troops to desegregate schools. He said at the time:

> I have been informed by various lawyers that the power does exist but, I can't imagine any set of circumstances that would ever induce me to send Federal troops into a Federal court and into any area to enforce the orders of a Federal court, because I believe that the common sense of America will never require it. Now, there may be that kind of authority resting somewhere, but certainly I am not seeking any additional authority of that kind, and I would never believe that it would be a wise thing to do in this country!

Along with other top staff members, I had just gone up to Newport, Rhode Island, to join the President when the Little Rock crisis broke. The President and Mrs. Eisenhower were there on a "working vacation." In an effort to avoid a head-on collision between himself and Faubus, the President agreed to see the governor at Newport. At the meeting Faubus agreed to recognize federal law and accepted the President's insistence that immediate action be taken to permit the Black students to attend school. Faubus returned to Little Rock and double-crossed the President. The guard was not removed. A wild, undisciplined mob threatened the Black students, and classes were canceled when a federal injunction removed the Arkansas troops.

The President issued a statement denouncing the "disgraceful occurrence" and warned that if the situation continued, he would use "whatever force may be necessary" to implement the court's order. The next morning, Mayor Woodrow Wilson Mann of Little Rock petitioned the President to send federal troops to disperse the mob which ranged out of control ". . . in the interest of Humanity, Law and Order, and because of Democracy world wide . . ." A state of anarchy existed in

Little Rock. Faubus had defied the Presidency, the Constitution, and impelled the President, even against his innate conviction not to resort to force, to send a thousand paratroopers from the 101st Airborne Division to take control of the area. The integration of Central High School was thus accomplished by federal force and the Black students entered the school under armed guard for the rest of the year.

Chapter Twenty-two

Among the mail on my desk upon my return from Africa was an invitation for us from the President and Mrs. Eisenhower to an evening reception planned for Queen Elizabeth and Prince Philip of England for October 17, 1957. That was quite a day in our house. Catherine was just back from Chicago, where she'd been closing her former home and arranging to have her furniture shipped east and she was in a very natural state of excitement about our invitation to the Royal reception. This would be my first time at an evening affair of this kind. A single person just can't function effectively at such parties; wives are a vital part of the social scheme in Washington, so all evening I found myself glowing with appreciation of my marital status!

The guests assembled in the ground floor reception room to await the summons upstairs. We were aware that we were in some kind of spotlight, being the only Blacks present and most of the guests knew that my wife was a recent bride. We walked into the reception room with a heavy sense of responsibility. I was thankful that I knew many of the guests and many on the staff were quick to bring their wives around for introductions and to offer congratulations.

We walked up the beautiful marble steps from the ground floor to the first floor foyer where the Marine Corps Band was playing and we moved through the Red Room into the Blue Room. The President, the Queen, Mrs. Eisenhower, and Prince Philip were standing on a slightly raised platform, receiving the guests. Each man preceded his wife and gave his name to the military aide who in turn gave it to the President, who passed it on to the Queen. The President spotted me, even before the military aide could get my name and in typical Eisenhower fashion said: "Hello there! This is the first time I've seen you since your marriage. Congratulations!"

The Queen was smiling at this, and when Catherine shook hands with the President he wished her happiness and told the Queen that she was a new bride. Mrs. Eisenhower received her in a manner that affected Catherine deeply, saying, "Oh, yes, this is the bride. You are radiant tonight! I want to welcome you, my dear, and wish you every possible happiness." After shaking hands with Philip, we went to the East Room where the musicale was to be held.

After all the guests were received, the Queen came into the East Room on the arm of the President and Mrs. Eisenhower on the arm of the Prince, and they sat in front of a small platform. Fred Waring's Pennsylvanians gave a forty-minute program that was a combination of American folk songs, patriotic airs, and songs about holidays that have been developed in this country over many years. It concluded with the "Battle Hymn of the Republic," one of the President's favorites. Then we all stood up, and the President said, "Good night, friends," and left with the royal guests.

We went into the State Dining Room for a buffet champagne supper. This was an opportunity to exchange greetings with staff members and other friends, and it was a pleasant hour. The Vice President and Mrs. Nixon were particularly glad to greet Catherine, and told her that they were very fond of her husband. The Vice President quipped: "Keep your eye on him and make him stay in line." She got a big kick out of this. He also said, "We couldn't get to your wedding, but we hope to see you real soon." The good-nights were friendly, and many people came up to say how happy they were to meet my wife and that they looked forward to seeing us socially.

Chapter Twenty-three

The pressures of the job both inside and outside of the White House began to swell. I began hating to go to the office. The letters and phone calls were mostly from irate friends and citizens who were fed up with the President's moderate stand on civil rights and allied problems. They accused him of refusing to assume the moral leadership of the country, and with resolution and affirmative speech to take a stand on the side of justice and human rights.

I felt self-conscious and foolish in my speeches throughout the country trying to defend the administration's record on civil rights. It was true that the administration had made more significant appointments than any other in recent history and that gestures had been made—such as sending troops into Little Rock to maintain law and order so that all children could go to school, but there was no strong, clarion, commanding voice from the White House righteously indignant over the plight of 18 million citizens who were fighting for their God-given rights of human dignity and self-determination.

For over a week, I would awake each morning with the opening lines of James Russell Lowell's "The Present Crisis" ringing in my ears:

> Once to every man and nation
> Comes the moment to decide . . .

Those lines written over a century ago were telling me that the time had come to decide once and for all what I was going to do about remaining on the job.

I argued with myself over what seemed to be the problem. I had voluntarily come into the job with my eyes open. Didn't I expect abuse and slander in a political set up? Yes. Didn't I expect disagreement and bitter opposition to some administration policies? Yes. Did I expect the President was going to champion Black rights at every turn? No. Did I expect to be popular with Black people because of my position in the White House? No. What then?

First of all, any Negro who is worth his right to life must look at every vital question from two sides—first as a Black, and then as an American. This double responsibility is a heavy stone upon anyone who must make a decision in a dual society. Always in the back of my mind was the incontrovertible fact that after all this pomp and ceremony was over, I would have to return to a Black community to live out my days. If in the eyes of this expectant, exacting, demanding group, I had not planted the race's flag high on the mountaintop of uncompromising citizenship, I would be an exile and a leper. How can one be loyal to two opposing responsibilities!

Early on Monday morning, October 21, 1957, the White House called me, announcing that Sherman Adams wanted to talk to me. In his typical fashion—without saying hello, or any other preliminary—he asked me: "Fred, how much of your time do you give to your job?" I was trying to think what he was driving at, and said that my job consumed a great deal of time. He said: "Well, maybe you won't be able to do what I have in mind but I wish you would talk to Arthur Larson about it. We're thinking about making you an assistant to Larson in his new post." Having no idea what Larson was going to do, I tried to beg off, but Adams would have none of it and told me to talk to him after I had talked to Larson. This was very disquieting. I had established a routine in my office, things were going well, and I had no desire to change positions or situations.

I went over to the United States Information Agency to see Larson in the afternoon. He had just resigned his position as director of USIA and the President had appointed him a special assistant on the White House staff. The newspapers had indicated that Larson would probably be engaged in international fields—perhaps in psychological warfare—but no one knew for sure exactly what his new assignment would be. He confided in me that he was to become the principal speech writer for the President, establishing a White House speech-writing section manned by himself and two assistants. The idea was to develop an agency that could collect material for speeches and then write them in such a fashion that the President would appear able and scholarly whenever he had a pronouncement to make.

The old hodgepodge method of developing presidential speeches was out. Under that system, the President had first accepted invitations to speak and it would later be decided what area he would cover. For example, if the speech was to be about agriculture, the Secretary of Agriculture would send rough notes over to the White House for possible use in the speech. If it was to be about civil rights, the Attorney General's office would offer suggestions. Various staff members versed in these subjects would try their hands at developing certain segments of the speech. There was always a mad rush to make the deadline and each speech had to pass through a half dozen hands before it was ready to go to the President for his approval.

Larson's idea was to have on hand up-to-date material and rough drafts on all vital subjects on which the President might wish to speak. For example, a speech developed on civil rights would be ready when the proper occasion arose. In other words, except in national or international crises, the subject matter of the speech would determine when the President spoke.

Larson told me that they had scoured the country but had not come up with anyone they felt was suited for the job. He said that he had collected all my speeches over a period of two years, read them, and had the feeling that I was just the man he needed to assist him. I told him that *I* felt he needed a professional speech writer. He said no, that what the job called for was a person who had a spiritual feeling about the President and the administration—someone who was truly saturated with this atmosphere and who knew the President as a man and was dedicated to him. I was the one for the job.

All this was flattering, but I had no desire to accept. My position in the White House had been unique. To Black Americans, I was a symbol of achievement. The Black press watched every move I made, and would be the first to question my move from Administrative Officer in the President's office to a job as assistant to a presidential special assistant. Even though the White House called this a promotion, it would be difficult to explain to my public.

There were other factors. Every Black delegation of any consequence that had come to Washington wanted to come to the White House to see me. I welcomed these opportunities to get to know such groups better and to have them get to know me. It had been possible to meet them in my offices because of the spaciousness of the Executive Office Building offices but the new Larson setup would have only a small cubbyhole in the East Wing of the White House.

On my own I had been putting out a lot of "brush fires" around the country during the past two years, as well as making scores of speeches. The new job would be a confining one.

I argued all of this out with Larson and Andy Goodpaster, but neither of them would budge. They indicated that it had been decided at the highest possible level that I would take the job. This put an end to all discussion. I moved into this new post with great trepidation and hoped that I would be pleasantly surprised by the outcome.

Chapter Twenty-four

My first move after the decision to become an aide to Arthur Larson was to call my old friend and mentor, Dr. William J. Barnes of Great Barrington, Massachusetts. All my adult life he had been my friend, father confessor, and benefactor. His beautiful estate in the Berkshires had been my refuge and sanctuary during the difficult years since the war. I had always gone there when vital questions plagued my soul and it was there I would go now to get his help in coming to grips with my stubborn problems.

I spent a long weekend at "Point of View," the Barnes's place. There in the quietude and placidity of rolling woods with an ax in my hand I literally carved out a course of future action, and chopped down all the little obstacles in my head that were barring the way to peace of mind and firm decision.

I resolved to stay on at the White House. The opportunity to serve both a President and one's race had never before come to a Black American. It might be a long time in coming again. To put personal difficulties above even the little good that might flow from this relationship would be cowardice. However, the real clincher in the decision was this—it was a struggle to get there and the opposition was severe. It was quite possible that if I resigned, no similar appointment would be made. The administration was not obligated by personal pledge to any other Black. Also, my very presence on the staff did some good. While many things were not done despite my presence, it did prevent some anti-Black acts from being attempted. Also, as long as I remained, there would always be a pipeline to the President and the top members of government. As to my present and future standing with members of my own race, it was out of my hands. I could only hope that they would recognize my efforts to chart a sensible, sane course in a position with little choice.

I further resolved that I could never be disloyal to Dwight Eisenhower. Despite his myopic view on civil rights, he was straining every nerve to serve to the best of his ability the interest and the welfare of all the people of the United States. In every decision he had to estimate what was best for all the people, and while he should show concern and deep interest in the ignoble plight of 10 percent of the population, his ultimate decisions had to be based on what he determined was best for the welfare of the whole. To me, this was a fair and honorable point of view which in no way dismissed the President's derelictions as regards the Black.

For a minority member in this kind of spot anywhere, there is always the haunting specter that to quit gives delight and comfort to one's enemies and oppressors. It indicates that you could not take it. It makes the anti-Blacks line up more solidly against any newcomer and the opposition become more active and determined.

I left Barnes's woods determined to continue to press for what I believed was right, and never to compromise with conscience or principle on my race's basic aspirations for human dignity and human rights. I would prefer to be fired for aggressiveness and forthrightness, rather than resign because my petitioning had fallen on deaf ears.

Chapter Twenty-five

My first assignment in my new job as assistant speech writer was to assist in writing the President's State of the Union Message for 1958, which was to be delivered on January 9. On the first of November, I made the physical shift of my office from the Executive Office Building to the East Wing of the White House.

As late as November 10, Mr. Larson had not spoken to me at any length about what he expected me to do. He did, however, hand me a portfolio containing departmental and Cabinet officer's reports on their functions, and this material was to be culled, sieved, and developed for the State of the Union Address.

Heretofore, it had taken scores of persons to develop the State of the Union Message. It was a tedious, confining, alarming task. The major problem was not what to put in, but what could judiciously be left out.

On November 25, the President suffered a chill on his return from meeting the King of Morocco at the airport, and his doctor ordered him to bed immediately. He had to miss a State dinner for the King, and the Vice President acted as host in his stead, escorting Mrs. Eisenhower to dinner. Any illness of the world's number one statesman throws foreign relations into a tailspin. The stock market reacted wildly, and there was a general feeling of anxiety and dismay throughout the nation.

At 4:00 P.M. on November 26, the latest bulletin on the President's health confirmed that he had apparently suffered a slight stroke. There seemed to be confusion in the exact diagnosis but the bulletin indicated that he had suffered a speech impairment although it had improved in the past twenty-four hours. For the next few days there was much editorial comment and feature writing about the President's illness, with much speculation as to whether the President would resign.

At the White House, all officials tried to maintain an outward calm, but all were deeply affected by this latest illness. The senior staff felt certain that if the President determined that he was not physically able to carry on in a satisfactory manner, he would resign. His complete honesty and dedication to his country would make him think long and hard about his duty. With the medical bulletins indicating that complete rest was the primary need at the moment, we all hoped and prayed that this would solve the situation. It did. He made a miraculous recovery!

On January 7, 1958, I was no better informed about the State of the Union Message than I had been two months before. Other than digesting and assembling material, I had not been given an opportunity to take part in its development in any way. There was great fanfare when I was given the assignment and both staff members, press, and friends thought I was working on it. Daily the staff members would ask me how it was going, and I was always embarrassed to reply, "I don't know."

Arthur Larson was neither staff-minded nor staff-oriented. He kept everything to himself and never took his co-workers into his confidence. Apparently, the State of the Union

Message was to be his personal version and he didn't want an assist from anyone.

At no time since I had been on the White House Staff had I been as discouraged and at such a low ebb about my status. This assignment had been promised as my most challenging—and it was turning out to be most disturbing and humiliating. Sherman Adams called me to his office one morning during this period to discuss an official matter and in the course of the conversation asked me how I was getting along. I told him that the job had failed to produce the "challenge" that he intimated in the beginning, and that apparently Mr. Larson was a "lone wolf" operator who did not confide in his colleagues. The Governor said he understood that was the way Mr. Larson worked, and that he felt I should "have it out with him."

This advice offered cold comfort to me. No matter how I felt about the matter, Larson at the moment was bogged down with the responsibility of getting out the speech and this was not the time to approach him with my complaint. However, as soon as the President's message had been delivered, I intended to get an official clarification on my status and what it was to be in the future.

Early in January 1958, Joseph V. Baker of Philadelphia, a Republican party stalwart of many years and prominent public relations man, came to Washington to see me. For many years, Baker had been handling race relations for the Railroad Association of America, United States Steel, and the Radio Corporation of America. He had the ear and confidence of some of the most powerful men and some of the largest contributors to the Republican party. Whatever he had to say was worth listening to.

He stated that Republicans all over the country were alarmed about the way the party had disintegrated. There was a feeling that the President had lost his grip because he could not be a candidate for reelection. A great many people felt that the President had no sense of politics at all and constantly weakened the party because he would not use his power to chastise those who stepped off the reservation. Then Baker stated that the attorney general's recent declaration that he did not propose to offer any civil rights legislation in the present

Congress and that there would be a cooling-off period on the whole problem of civil rights, had infuriated most Blacks throughout the country. He added that Blacks felt that I had "sold them down the river," because, despite my protestations that I was not the President's advisor on minority problems, I could not escape the moral responsibility of failing to go to bat for my race. The President had made many blunders in race relations and it was incredible that a Black could be on his staff and permit him to stumble so badly.

Baker felt that the Republicans had done me an injustice by not giving wider publicity to my actual role in the White House. He added that, at the moment, in the eyes of many Blacks I was a traitor and would have to work very hard to overcome this disadvantage before leaving the White House. I was shocked beyond belief! I was aware that the Negro press had been somewhat unfriendly to me. This had been understandable because a member of the Negro Publishers Association had castigated me publicly for ". . . not giving the Black press any tips . . ."

This blast from Baker nearly destroyed my spirit and made a gaping hole in my heart. My sole effort up to now had been to try to convince the President and other high officials that if a Black person with proper background, character, and training was given an opportunity, he could measure up as well as any other American under the same circumstances. My job was to serve the President in the capacity to which he had appointed me. It was neither feasible nor wise for me to try to advise him on anything outside of the scope of my responsibilities unless he requested it. It must have been perfectly apparent to Sherman Adams, the President, and any other member of the administration, that if for no other reason than the fact that I was Black, I had the ability to advise them on matters that affected the Black race. The fact that they sought and obtained this advice and information from others, while it was of deep concern to me, was not within my power to alter or change.

The month of February, 1958 was spent in California. The idea behind the trip was to permit me to make several speeches in that state which would give impetus to Republican activity. It was a stimulating trip. Catherine accompanied me and we went by train so that we could enjoy the beauty of the western states in this country. I was not interested in promoting any particular candidate. I merely wanted to make the people aware of the administration's program in various phases of national life.

The minority leader of the Senate was Robert Knowland of California who was relinquishing his Senate seat to run for governor. Rumor had it that he was making this move because he felt it would be an easier springboard to the Republican nomination for the Presidency in 1960. Upon my arrival in San Francisco, I was surprised to find sentiment among minorities running steadily against Senator Knowland. He was particularly unpopular among Blacks. The Black community was greatly surprised when the Oakland paper owned by the Senator's family gave me front-page prominence.

I had been told by Black leaders that Knowland family attitudes toward Blacks were more condescending than earnest. This situation was prevalent among white Republican leaders in their relationship with Black leaders or voters. There was a paternalistic attitude and Black politicians did as they were told. In most instances, minority leadership had been chosen by whites and the selection had been made on the issues of the person's ineffectiveness rather than ability. This method had been used for fifty years before when Blacks had less intellectual capacity to choose for themselves. At this time the method was an insult and only led to indignation and a loss of votes.

It was difficult for the heads of the Republican party in California to accept the fact that I was a presidential assistant and should be accorded the same respect and courtesies that would be extended to anyone from the president's staff. They were prepared to accept me as a "Negro assistant" who was sent merely to chit-chat with Negroes to give them a feeling of achievement. I refused to accept this role and this made many Republican officials uncomfortable and rude.

At my first press conference at the St. Francis Hotel in San Francisco, a public relations man from the Republican State Central Committee was sent to my room fifteen minutes before the meeting to tell me what to say! I dismissed him as courteously as I could, but intimated that this was a distinct insult to a member of the president's staff whose daily responsibilities made contact with the press a routine matter.

This same racial situation existed in Los Angeles, a big sprawling country town with a Black population then of over 300,000. There was a colony of extremely wealthy Blacks in Los Angeles but the great bulk was leaderless and without a respected voice. Hence, as in countless other cities, the Republican party was missing a great bet. Given adequate opportunity for participation in party circles and opportunity for leadership expression, these Blacks would become a great bulwark of strenght to the party. An example of the irony of this situation was that James Roosevelt, eldest son of the former President, was a congressional candidate in a district where he did not live and where more than a majority of the residents were nonwhite.

The Republicans had selected a brilliant young Black lawyer, Crispus Wright, to oppose Roosevelt but denied him adequate funds and tacit support from the white leadership of the party to wage an earnest campaign.

I tried to do what I could to put new life in the movement and to challenge the people to greater effort. It was a difficult time to appear on Republican platforms. We had to admit we were in some kind of recession and there was ominous unemployment all about. In every question-and-answer session after a speech I was attacked, rather than questioned, on the fact that the Republicans had sat by and let the country drop off into another recession. Republicans who had enjoyed Eisenhower's prosperity for years were the most bitter in their denunciation of him. This sort of thing made these public appearances difficult and unhappy and I returned to Washington after three weeks, tired and disconsolate.

Ten days after I returned from California, I decided to "go to the mat" with Sherman Adams on my future status on the White House staff. I sent the governor a memo requesting a conference with him at the earliest possible moment. He replied by phone asking what he could do for me. I had hoped to avoid talking on the phone about a personal problem, but this is the way he coped with shortage of time.

I told him that in view of the fact that nothing had

developed in my case, I would like his permission to return to my former position as Administrative Officer for Special Projects. The Governor said he had decided I was needed out in the field to make more speeches. I replied that I had been doing just that, but to continue it I needed some kind of defined White House status and a valid title. He suggested that I take the matter up with Andy Goodpaster and after that the three of us would sit down together and discuss the whole situation.

I immediately called Goodpaster and requested an appointment. He told me to come right over. Again I went over the situation with him and said that my position was now a subject for discussion among even messengers and White House employees. It was just a question of time before the matter became public property and we would be forced to answer questions from the press. Goodpaster agreed that something should be done immediately. He reiterated his conviction that, if at all possible, I should not return to my old assignment, as it would imply a defeat. The speechmaking and speechwriting assignments were supposed to have been an advance and going back would be difficult to explain.

I made it very clear to him that I was not interested in "made work." I had not volunteered to come to the White House but had been invited. The present situation was not of my own doing but had been brought about by someone else. I did not want him or anyone to feel that they had created something for me because I was "the President's boy." I was quite willing to pit my abilities and qualifications against anyone on the staff and I wanted a responsible job of some consequence based on ability and merit. Short of this, I was not interested. He said he would dig into the matter and let me know.

The next ten days were eventful ones in the White House. There were several changes made in job designations—including my own—which surprised and shook up many people. I finally got the call from General Goodpaster informing me that he and Sherman Adams had decided that it would be best for me to return to my former position in the President's Executive Office.

I returned to my old suite of offices in the Executive Office

Building and was happy to be back in those spacious quarters. It had been interesting having offices in the East Wing of the White House, but they had been small and cramped. Also, I was back with my former secretary "Junior" (Mary O'Madigan) and brought along Peggy King with me from the East Wing as a new addition to the staff. Once more we had a very effective team—and while the job might get rougher—we expected busy and rewarding times together in our familiar surroundings.

January 27, 1958 was a banner day for me. After almost five years in the White House, I finally received my commission duly signed by the President and attested to by the Secretary of State. I was officially sworn into my job by the President's counsel, Gerry Morgan, at 10:30 A.M. in his office. My wife and my three secretaries were present as well as three or four White House staffers who just happened to drop into Morgan's office unaware of what was happening.

This event marked the end of a long hard fight to receive proper recognition for my assignment on the President's staff. Even this swearing-in was not done in the usual style or manner. The President usually attended the swearing-in of any of his staff officers, but he was not present at mine. Why? The White House was a little embarrassed about me. I should have been commissioned four years earlier when I first came aboard. But to have handled this current event in the usual manner would have opened a Pandora's box of questions and difficult answers.

If the President had attended, the press would have been there, and there would have to have been some explanations as to why I was going back to the same job with the same title, and yet was being officially commissioned and sworn in. To avoid all this confusion and embarrassment, I agreed to a modest ceremony.

Chapter Twenty-six

In between the hectic pace of events in my White House assignment there were happenings in my personal life from time to time that provided an added dimension of human interest. I had told a few friends of my desire to find a suitable position for myself when my tour of duty was over in Washington and asked them to keep a look out. Tom Stephens, Presidential Appointment Secretary, encouraged me and tried to utilize his friendship with some of the prominent businessmen in the country to help me pick up leads. Tom experienced the same difficulty I had. Many leading businessmen were aghast when it was suggested that a Black be offered a position of consequence or influence in their organizations. A number of them still thought in terms of "boy," and this attitude had not changed very much since the Civil War. Despite my White House status, it was incredible to many of them that my job consisted of anything more than being a glorified messenger boy or a political sop to attract Black voters.

Tom made an appointment for me to see one of the most prominent lawyers in Washington, a personal friend of the President whose clients included Coca-Cola and other Fortune 500 corporations. Tom had sent this man a note about me asking his assistance in helping me pick up leads. The lawyer, whom I shall call "Mr. Jones," had me come to his office at 8:45 A.M.. He told me he had played golf with Sherman Adams the day before and that the governor had spoken very highly of me. From his opening sentence, however, I was aware that Mr. Jones had no conception of my desires, abilities, or present position. He asked me what my salary was and when I told him he was shocked! He had no idea that Blacks made more than fifty dollars a week and he asked me point blank if I believed that such a fabulous salary would continue after I left the White House. He then proceeded to lecture me on the devilment of the 1954 Supreme Court decision on Civil Rights. He felt that it was a sad mistake that had merely increased race conflict in this country and caused white men of his generation to become more embittered. As a result, they were teaching their children that integration must never happen.

It was difficult for him to believe that I had worked for CBS and it was also difficult for him to accept my education. He had originally wanted to help but he had been thinking in terms of my having some kind of job that "a *nice* colored boy" would have. He wanted to know if I would be interested in selling second-hand automobiles to "colored people." He said that Coca-Cola had hired three "colored boys" here in Washington to do some public relations work for them and that their principal job was to keep Black dealers happy. "However," he said, "these three boys combined don't make the salary you make now."

By this time I was feeling ill and decided to conclude the interview by telling him I appreciated his seeing me and felt he had given me enough of his expensive time. He said he would keep trying to think of helpful ideas and would see me again. I left his office thoroughly shaken, discouraged, and bitter. I had hoped that despite many hateful past experiences, strides were being made, particularly in business and industry, so that a person could be accepted on the basis of ability. Apparently this was not true. Mr. Jones in his southern drawl had indicated to me that it would be a long time—if ever—before racial bias would vanish in America; that one would have to work and be accepted as a Black and not as an American who had something to offer his employer.

In the past months I had thanked the Almighty a thousand times for my beautiful and wise wife, Catherine. She is intelligent, well traveled, well educated, and instinctively did the right thing at the right time. Upon her arrival in Washington she was very careful about accepting social invitations, not wanting to create the impression that she was overly eager to share in functions given by the wives of White House staff or official Washington.

One day she went to a luncheon given for the White House wives by Mrs. Amos Peaslee at historic Gunston Hall on the Potomac. Mrs. Peaslee was one of Washington's most distinguished hostesses and a regent of Gunston Hall. Her husband was Deputy Special Assistant to the President. When the invitation had come, I expressed reservations about Catherine's acceptance. Gunston Hall was in Virginia and that state had oppressive laws about socializing between the races. It could actually be a penal offense for Blacks and whites to socialize in Virginia. Concerned about this aspect, without Catherine's knowledge I called Mrs. Sherman Adams to ask her if she felt Catherine would have any difficulty. I told Mrs. Adams that I was used to rebuffs and insults and was hardened to them, but that Catherine had led a very sheltered life, brought up in an atmosphere of culture and good breeding. While I never doubted her ability to handle any situation, I did not want her to be hurt by discourteous people. Rachel Adams immediately invited Catherine to go with her. Mrs. Adams, as the "Third Lady" of the nation, could brook any rude situation or person.

Catherine had a very interesting time at the affair. Her experience duplicated many of mine. The wives who were socially secure were kind and friendly. The socially insecure—because of personal backgrounds or their husbands' average positions—were unfriendly and nervous. During the luncheon, some of the women, intrigued by the historic surroundings of Gunston Hall, began to tell about their own ancestors trying to establish themselves as having roots deep in American culture and history. Catherine innocently asked how far Gunston Hall was from Gordonsville, Virginia. She was asked why Gordonsville would be of interest to her. She replied that it was the birthplace of her father, that she had been born a Gordon, and that the town was named after her family. (Her father's people were the bankers and merchants of that historic area.)

Amazement and incredulity gripped the group. It was immediately apparent that this woman had some of the bluest blood of Virginia in her veins and despite her copper-colored skin, had as much right as anyone to claim herself an FFV. The information put a decided chill on the ladies at her, and surrounding, tables.

In the evening at dinner at home, we would always review our experiences during the day and, calling upon our sense of humor, would try to take the sting out of situations like Gunston Hall. However, each episode like this took a great deal out of me. There was never an opportunity to relax completely; one was always on display. If you were completely relaxed, it looked like presumption, and to be too reserved looked like snobbishness.

I felt that Catherine by overcoming her shyness and continuing to represent me and our race at these functions was making a wonderful contribution to democracy in official Washington. I felt she had to try to pave the way among women for an understanding of what tolerance really meant.

On the night of April 24, 1958, I was watching the 11:00 P.M. news on television when the startling announcement was made that Maxwell Rabb had just tendered his resignation as secretary of the cabinet. All night I tried to puzzle who would handle the delicate and vexatious portfolios of Civil Rights and Negro Affairs. Maxwell had handled these problems for the President since the beginning of his administration in 1953.

Early the next morning Sherman Adams summoned Max and me to his office and in his typically terse and unemotional manner said to me: "The President has agreed that from this point you will handle all correspondence and problems coming into the White House dealing with Civil Rights and Negro Affairs." *That was all!*

There was tremendous irony about this whole situation. After the President was nominated in 1952 and there were discussions on who would accompany him to the White House, I *refused* point blank to be his advisor on Black affairs. I said I would only go to Washington to assist him if I were given the same recognition, responsibilities, and privileges of any other staff members. There was something abhorrent to me in being a professional "race-saver." However, when Rabb resigned, with the exception of our unsettled relations with the Russians, there was no problem that gave the administration more concern or more anxious moments than civil rights. Max Rabb made my appointment and acceptance certain by his observation to both the President and Sherman Adams that it would be discrimination in reverse if they did not turn this responsibility over to the staff member who had the ability, knowledge and tact to handle it.

I went back to my office, closed the door, and got on my knees to pray. I got up having resolved that one of the prime requirements of first-class citizenship was to put race and color in their true perspective and estimate all problems and situations from the standpoint of an American. I would try to rid myself of all personal emotions and make a cold-blooded analysis of every situation in order to give the best possible advice to the President of the United States.

I went to the farewell luncheon for Rabb at the Press Club given by his many friends in Washington. The high and the mighty were there, including the Vice President and Sherman Adams. There were hundreds of words of warm praise for his efforts during his term of office and friends presented him with an oil painting of himself by Dr. Oppenheim and a plaque expressing high sentiments. It was a warm and sentimental affair.

I knew and acknowledged that Max would be missed in the White House. Although I did not always agree with his methods and actions in handling minority group affairs, he had been pioneering in a difficult and complex field. He had a high code of ethics, and was certainly an honest man of great integrity. There were times when his soul was sorely tried by pressures from within and without. But I must confess that he was perhaps the only person on the White House staff who showed deep personal concern about the plight of minorities in the country.

Chapter Twenty-seven

It was clear to me that if the pressures on the White House from the Black press and social action groups were to be blunted and quieted, representatives of these groups would have to have more direct access to the President. They should be able to talk with him, ask questions, and receive answers.

With this in mind, I took charge of the petition from the Negro Publishers Association for the President to address a "summit meeting" of 400 Negro leaders from across the country, meeting in Washington on May 13th. The President consented to address an afternoon meeting.

A week before, I had sent to the President a short "fact sheet" for his use in developing remarks. I had warned against the use of the term "you people," which is anathema to Blacks, because it sets them apart from the body politic and makes them "different" from other citizens.

Jim Hagerty and I accompanied the President to the meeting. In his typically honest manner, the President told the assembly that, while laws should not be ignored in bestowing citizenship rights upon Americans, it had to be acknowledged that prejudice because of race and color is deeply rooted in the hearts of people and can only be changed by education and by constant work on the part of enlightened citizens. Taking off his reading glasses and tossing aside his notes the President continued: ". . . *But you people must be patient and use forbearance in your efforts to gain citizenship privileges.*"

The audience reacted as if a time bomb had exploded. Their contorted and pained faces expressed their disbelief and disdain. Sitting on the platform next to the President, I could feel life draining from me, and I wished I could escape without walking through the auditorium crowd. When we had come in an hour before, the applause had been thunderous. When we left it sounded like a few people with gloves on were clapping hands. We walked out through a scornful, insulted audience. We rode back to the White House in almost total silence.

I attended the evening meeting of the same group because I wanted to take my lumps in person, and possibly be interviewed at the site regarding my reactions to the President's speech. The vituperative damning of me by several editors was bitter gall to take. Roy Wilkins of the NAACP devoted a great part of his address to the denunciation of the President's conservative attitude on civil rights and other speakers fanned the flames of a "call-to-arms" against an inept and spineless administration.

During the next few weeks, a reign of terror embraced the rural South. Clennon King, a Black college professor, attempted to enroll in the University of Mississippi to work on his Ph.D. He was escorted from the university by the state police and committed to a psychiatric hospital on the grounds that he must have been insane to presume that he could attend the school. The nation's reaction to this was swift and gratifying. The President's mail became heavy with letters and telegrams from white and Black citizens imploring him to take some action to protect the civil rights of Clennon King.

Another explosive and terrifying incident occurred in Terrell County, Georgia. In the little town of Dawson, a plantation section of the state, news stories revealed that several

Blacks had been killed without provocation in the past weeks and that conditions were worse than those in Nazi-occupied countries during World War II. The chief of police in an interview related that terror was necessary in order to keep "niggers" in their place, and killing a few of them once in a while was always good medicine for the rest of them.

John W. Dobbs of Atlanta, Grand Master of the Negro Masons in Georgia, had written me before the newspaper exposé, begging me to request the President to take some action to stop the horrible brutality going on in Terrell County. It was a bizarre story of Blacks having their eyes beaten out and their skulls crushed for no apparent reason. It seemed that this was an accepted sport for the local police. Dobbs attached copies of letters from ministers in the area who gave pitiful reports of the need for federal intervention in order to save the lives of the people there. They told the story of one lad who was viciously beaten and later died merely because he had begged the police officers not to pistol-whip his father. The ministers went on to say that it was even dangerous for their members to go to church at night because the police would prey upon the communicants. They said that if the FBI or someone could not help at once, it would be necessary for them to get out their shot guns and resolve to die trying to protect their own families.

Upon receipt of Dobbs's letter, I went over to Attorney General Rogers's office to consult with the Assistant Attorney General in charge of Civil Rights. His coolness and non-chalance about the whole matter disturbed me to no end. I realized that in his spacious air-conditioned office, he could not visualize the desperate situation of the poor devils who had asked me for help. The FBI had been gathering reports but apparently the federal government had no intention of inter-fering. I knew that in many cases the federal government could not enter unless it could be proved that some federal statute had been violated, but in this instance there was *prima facie* evidence that civil rights were being ignored and that Blacks were suffering wanton brutality at the hands of con-scienceless police officers. Their rights and privileges as citizens were being denied without due process of law.

I pleaded with the assistant attorney general to do all in his power to bring some kind of pressure to bear to stop this brutality. I then called Mr. Dobbs to tell him what I had done expressing the hope that some action would result from my visit to the attorney general's office. I will never forget his choked voice, thanking me for moving so swiftly and telling me what harrowing days there had been in Terrell County.

With an epidemic of police brutality, maimings, and killings happening all along the southern front. Dr. Martin Luther King, Jr., continued his petitioning to the President for a meeting with Black leaders at the White House. Dr. King was asked to come to the White House to discuss his request with Rocco Siciliano, Special Assistant to the President for Personnel Management, and me. At the meeting a member of the attorney general's office was also present.

Dr. King pointed out that with the schools closed for the summer, this was the strategic time for the President to meet with Black leaders and talk about the future of integrated schools in the country as provided for in the Supreme Court decision in 1954. King felt that the signs that Virginia would oppose the court order to integrate schools in Arlington and similar indications in other places could lead to serious rioting and perhaps bloodshed in the fall. To effect plans to meet the situation, he thought the President ought to have a free, honest, and factual discussion with leading Blacks.

Siciliano and I agreed that such a meeting should be held, but who would be the invitees? This was always a sore point. Many knowledgeable persons believed themselves to be "Black leaders" in some area and candidates for any meeting where the future of the race was being discussed. I realized Roy Wilkins of the NAACP should be present, but I was keenly aware that he was in the "dog house" because of his forceful attack upon the President during his speech before the summit conference of Negro leaders in Washington in early May. However, Dr. King made it very clear that it would be unthinkable for him to come to the White House without Wilkins, and that it would be difficult to explain why Wilkins was not included in such a conference. We all agreed that A. Philip Randolph must be present at the conference because he was a respected citizen in whom most Americans had complete faith.

At a second meeting two weeks later Siciliano and I conferred again with Dr. King to firm up recommendations to be handed to the President. We agreed on a slate of those to be invited to the White House meeting with the President: A. Philip Randolph, Vice President of AFL-CIO and head of the Sleeping Car Porters Brotherhood; Roy Wilkins, Executive Secretary of the NAACP; Lester B. Granger, Executive Secretary of the National Urban League; and, Dr. Martin Luther King, Jr., President of the Southern Christian Leadership Conference.

The name of Congressman Adam Clayton Powell came up in the discussion. The President had already promised to see Congressman Powell sometime during the year, but a recent indictment for income tax problems by a Federal Grand Jury posed a delicate situation. If Powell came to the White House, critics would say he was there to make some kind of deal about his case. If he was not invited, his supporters would say that despite his support of the Administration (which had caused him to lose the support of his own party) the Administration was kicking him when he was down. Powell's possible attendance would have to be scrutinized and discussed at length top-side.

Rocco Siciliano and I spent several weeks trying to develop and complete all details for the President's meeting with the four national leaders. The President had finally consented to the meeting and when the news unofficially reached the Press, Rocco and I were presented with myriad headaches.

Our troubles began when the Black paper, the *New York Amsterdam News*, scooped all other papers in the country with a front page story on the coming meeting. They quoted an "unimpeachable source." As soon as the news spread through the country we began to receive requests from countless people who wanted to be part of the delegation. Even though I had an unlisted phone number, people somehow obtained the number and called me at home, night and day, pressing me to add this or that name to the delegation.

To make the situation a complete donnybrook, Representative Powell informed the press that the meeting was the result of his suggestions to the White House and that the persons named in the delegation were those he had urged the President to see. This created the impression that Powell was responsible for the decision and that he had named the representatives. This put the White House in a difficult spot so it became necessary for Jim Hagerty to rush a story into print to counteract Congressman Powell's claim.

Powell then sent a telegram to the White House demanding that a Black woman be added to the delegation. He was interested in a specific candidate who was president of the National Council of Negro Women. In addition to his telegram, many telephone calls were made, and this was the beginning of a barrage from prominent Blacks in all sections of the country. In order to make myself unavailable I left town for a long weekend. However, the "ole debil" followed me. A headline greeted me in New York: *"MORROW DISCRIMINATES AGAINST NEGRO WOMANHOOD!"*

The meeting with the President was cordial and A. Philip Randolph, the "Old Lion," did a masterful job. As he had done in meetings with Presidents since Franklin Roosevelt, he held the line, never wavered, and kept the right focus on the hard issues. One of the problems of greatest concern was the matter of a federal judge in Arkansas who had given the Little Rock Board of Education a stay of two and a half years before starting to integrate the school system there. If the stay was permitted to stand, it would mean that eight Black children who had already been admitted to Little Rock Central High School the year before would not be permitted to return, but would be sent to enroll in Black schools. This was a slap in the face as far as the Supreme Court decision was concerned, and there was a strong feeling at the meeting that the Federal District Court's decision had reflected personal bias rather than law.

This meeting was an historic one. Rather than depend upon my personal notes to give the facts and the flavor of that session, I have decided to present the "Memorandum For The White House Files" developed by Rocco C. Siciliano after the meeting. We both concurred in its content although he was the sole author. Also publicly presented for the first time is the historic "A Statement to President Dwight D. Eisenhower," signed by the conferees: A. Philip Randolph, Lester B. Granges, Reverend Martin Luther King, and Roy Wilkins.

June 24, 1958

MEMORANDUM FOR THE FILES

Subject: Meeting of Negro Leaders with the President—June 23, 1958

The President met with: Dr. Martin Luther King, Jr., President, Southern Christian Leadership Conference

A. Philip Randolph, International President, Brotherhood of Sleeping Car Porters

Roy Wilkins, President, NAACP

Lester B. Granger, Executive Secretary, National Urban League

Also present were Attorney General Rogers, E. Frederic Morrow, and myself.

After introductions, Mr. Randolph, as the spokesman, laid before the President the attached statement. He prefaced the written statement by commending the President strongly for the many efforts he has made to advance the political and economic status of the American Negro. He said that they would not be present at the meeting if they did not have the firm conviction that the President was a man of courage and integrity who had shown leadership and brought about accomplishment in this field. He spoke strongly and favorably about the President's action in the Little Rock episode. He then proceeded, beginning on page 4, to read the nine recommendations contained in the statement, including the closing paragraphs. Following this, he asked Dr. King to speak.

Dr. King said he wanted to comment about the first three of the recommendations and that, as a minister, he felt these recommendations were designed to help mobilize the emotions of the spirit which, in turn, would aid in the fight for abolishment of segregation. He said that a Presidential pronouncement as called for in the first recommendation would give a moral boost to the Nation. Speaking of the second recommendation, which calls for a White House conference, he is convinced, he said, as a southern Negro, that the social, political and economic reprisals which exist today in the South prevent the goodwill of white Southerners from being expressed. He felt such a conference would provide the forum for expressions of such goodwill. In urging action on the third recommendation, he said that wider dissemination of government information on this subject would provide the factual basis needed to educate further the communities and localities throughout the South and the Nation. He felt that without action along the lines of these three recommendations there would be a continuation of delaying tactics. He agreed that morals cannot be legislated (only education and religion can do this, he said) and that internal attitudes are hard to change, but that action is possible to attempt to control the external effects of such attitudes.

Mr. Wilkins emphasized the President's own record in the field of improvement of Negro rights, recalling the fact that Armed Services integration is now about complete, and that the President was responsible for the passage of the Civil Rights Bill last year. He then spoke on behalf of recommendation No. 4 and urged that the Administration seek again the inclusion of Part III which had been deleted during the heat of the debate last Fall. This is needed in order that more legal authority be provided the Attorney General. He said that the Justice Department was "inhibited, so it is reported" because they lack this necessary statutory authority. Wilkins then said he was "dismayed, distressed and angered" by the Lemley court decision of last Saturday. He said that the picture had been best described by a porter in New York City as he was leaving to come to Washington. The porter said that the decision has "given them a map," meaning that this decision has explained to the segregationists how best to proceed to defeat school integration. He then spoke of the necessity of protecting the right to vote, explaining that in one community in the South where a college was located, Negro faculty members with Masters and Doctors degrees were unable to qualify to vote because of the rigid tests administered by local registrars. He felt that when more Negroes were able to vote in the South this would bring about peaceable change and adjustment. He said that the right to vote was the "most effective and bloodless way" to solve this whole problem. He said that it was natural for a colored person who felt aggrieved in a local community to want to turn to Washington, the White House and the President for aid. He then related to the President an incident which occurred during the President's visit to Oklahoma City last Fall in which eight high school science scholarship winners were presented to the President. One of them was a colored girl, he said, for whom this would never have been possible if integration had not taken place in that city in recent years.

Mr. Granger recalled to the President that, in his lifetime, he has seen three different phases of Negro activity in the field of civil rights: during his World War I days, during the time of the depression, and today. He said he had not known a period when the bitterness of the Negro showed "more signs of congealing" than today. Mr. Granger continued, saying the Negro had been led to believe that there was hope and that progress was being made when, suddenly, it appears stopped. He said this was the reason for the reaction by the Negroes at last month's Summit meeting to the President's remarks, and because of which he assumed the President might be disappointed. He referred to Agnes Meyer's recent article in *The Atlantic Monthly*, calling her a person of "goodwill, even though not always of good judgment." He said that in this article she had "misquoted" (meaning misstated, I believe) the New York City School Board efforts. He said this type of article only brings about more confusion by well-meaning white people. He commended the kind of leadership exhibited by Dr. King in the South, who, he said, "kept alive a free spirit."

The Attorney General commented that the reason, in his mind, for any bitterness which might exist, is the very fact that progress is being made today, pointing out that in prior years speeches were made but progress did not follow, and so hope never really built up. Now, with the progress of the past recent years, some of the hopes have become realized; occasional setbacks or delays should be regarded only as temporary. Mr. Rogers said that we are defending the laws by aggressive court action whenever and wherever it appears that the legal facts are sufficient to bring them to a successful conclusion. He emphasized that it would be extremely unwise and damaging to institute court action in every individual complaint situation. He then said that he thought the statement lacked a *written* preface of the type which Mr. Randolph had just made *orally* (commending the accomplishments of this Administration) and gave no appearance of appreciation for the gains of recent years. He also recalled Mr. Wilkins' willingness to abandon Part III of the proposed Civil Rights Bill during the heat of last year's debate.

The President then spoke, saying that he was extremely

dismayed to hear that after 5½ years of effort and action in this field these gentlemen were saying that bitterness on the part of the Negro people was at its height. He wondered if further constructive action in this field would not only result in more bitterness.

Mr. Granger, seconded by Mr. Randolph and Mr. Wilkins, hastily assured the President that the bitterness they referred to was not directed to the President or the Administration but only to the communities in which apparent though slow progress was being made and then stopped: that the bitterness consisted of individual reactions to obstacles met.

The President spoke forcibly about the need for diligent and careful perusal by the Federal Government of any actions in this field. He did not comment in any way on the Judge Lemlay decision or the Little Rock affair. He said he did not propose to comment—and knew they did not expect him to—on the recommendations which he had before him, but said that he would obviously be glad to consider them. He then said that there might be at first blush some value in convoking a White House conference, but added that he was doubtful if it would be productive of anything.

Mr. Randolph answered this last observation by saying he thought the President might give it a high moral tone, to which the President replied there was only so much any President could do in opening such a meeting. Mr. Rogers agreed with the President and said this could only serve as a sounding board for the reaffirmation of previously announced positions by spokesmen (acknowledged and otherwise) in this area. Mr. Rogers emphasized again that the President had directed him to take aggressive actions in all matters affecting the Federal authority. The President agreed and then emphasized the importance of voting rights.

The meeting concluded with the President indicating his appreciation of meeting with the group.

In the press conference which followed the meeting, it appeared to me that the positions taken by the four leaders were basically very honest and favorable recitals of what had occurred at the meeting. The news accounts speak for themselves, but I took note of one significant question asked by Louis Lautier (only Negro member of the National Press Club Association) of Mr. Wilkins: he asked what had occurred in the meeting which had changed his attitude. He repeated this to mean Mr. Wilkins's attitude toward the President from the position taken a month ago by him. Mr. Wilkins was very indignant and didn't really respond to the question. Efforts were made to bait Wilkins in the press conference inasmuch as he seems to be the most militant of the group, but I would say that he held himself under control.

Rocco C. Siciliano

A STATEMENT TO PRESIDENT DWIGHT D. EISENHOWER

The process of peaceful advancement toward equality of citizenship for all Americans has reached a critical turn.

New economic and cultural forces in our nation's life are changing the pattern of Negro-white relations. Any effort to impede this process will affect unfavorably all American society. Frequently tension is an inherent element of basic social change. Thus it is not a matter of choice between an unjust status quo with social peace, and integration with tension. The nation can adopt forthrightly a bold program which moves through tension to a democratic solution; or it can depend upon evasion and compromise which purport to avoid tension, but which in reality lead the entire society toward economic, social, and moral frustration.

Years of educational, legislative, and legal efforts to bring the status of Negro Americans in line with the guarantees of the Constitution have led, inevitably, to the determination by our highest court that enforced racial segregation and its attendant discrimination in publicly-owned facilities is morally and legally indefensible.

At every intermediate stop along the way to this conclusion bitter opposition was encountered, but justice and common sense have heretofore prevailed; the unity of the nation has been strengthened; its moral fibre has been renewed.

Today, however, the last-ditch resistance to the application of principles long since accepted by most of the nation has assumed a significance beyond the question of racial justice, important as that is. The welfare of the whole country is involved in the issues with which this presentment is concerned.

Presently there is manifest a pattern of calloused disrespect for law. Moral values have been corrupted. Mob violence has emerged as an instrument to maintain the status quo.

The basic constitutional freedoms of speech, association, assembly, and redress of grievances, vital to all Americans, have been perverted, abridged, or denied through arbitrary practices or cynical legislation in the states.

State and local office holders of high and low station and national legislators, all sworn to uphold the Constitution, have incited to disobedience of the law and have campaigned nationally for support for their position. In community after community, fear of reprisals or of scorn has reduced to a whisper the reproach a moral people should feel for immoral behavior.

It is no secret that the foreign relations program of our nation has been hampered and damaged by the discriminatory treatment accorded citizens within the United States, solely on the basis of their race and color. In our world-wide struggle to strengthen the free world against the spread of totalitarianism, we are sabotaged by the totalitarian practices forced upon millions of our Negro citizens.

These citizens have exhibited unparalleled patience in the face of decades of proscription and persecution. They have placed unfaltering trust in the guarantees of the Constitution and in the orderly processes of the courts. Today they are frustrated and angry. In their resentment and despair, an increasing number of them are questioning whether their forbearance and respect for orderly procedure are rewarding.

The decision of Federal Judge Harry J. Lemlay reversing school integration in Little Rock and postponing further effort until 1961 has shocked and outraged Negro citizens and millions of their fellow Americans. This opinion is being construed, rightly or wrongly, as a green light to lawless elements in their defiance of Federal authority.

We have come to this pass largely because we have not recognized that adjustments of the magnitude called for in this vast social change cannot be undertaken effectively without planned effort of similar magnitude. We cannot combat pneumonia by prescribing an occasional tablet of aspirin and a goblet of goodwill.

Just as our Government has moved with pace and imagination to meet the revolution of rising expectations in other parts of the world, so it is essential that similar imagination and intelligence—and courage—be shown by our

Government in meeting the results of the revolution of rising expectations at home.

This is not to say that measures taken by this Administration up to now have been without value. The nation was immeasurably strengthened in its understanding of the gravity of the constitutional issues by the action taken at Little Rock last September to uphold the sanctity of the orders of Federal courts. The Chief Executive's personal support of efforts to eliminate segregation in the armed services and on service installations has been beneficial, although pockets still remain which should be wiped out. The enactment of the 1957 Civil Rights Act with the active support of the Administration was a significant advance.

Valuable as these and other measures have been, they have not as yet clearly provided a planned and integral approach to the multitude of tough problems which must be solved along the way. It is in the hope that these essential objectives may thereby be promoted that we suggest and urge the adoption of the following program:

1. The President of the United States should declare in a nationwide pronouncement, prior to September, that the law will be vigorously upheld with the total resources at his command.

2. Much emphasis has been laid on the need for restoring communication between white and colored Southerners who are troubled by a common fear of reaction. The President can well set the example in this matter by convoking a White House Conference of constructive leadership to discuss ways and means of complying peaceably with the Court's rulings.

3. Information, resources, and advice of the appropriate government agencies addressed to the problems of integration should be made available to all officials and community groups seeking to work out a program of education and action.

4. The President should request both parties to lay aside partisanship so that the Congress can enact a civil rights bill which will include Part III originally in the 1957 bill, in order that constitutional rights other than voting rights may be enforced by the United States Attorney General. Lack of adequate and clear statutory authority has made the Federal Government a mere spectator in the disgraceful maneuverings at Little Rock.

5. We urge the President to direct the Department of Justice to give all legal assistance possible under the law, including the filing of a brief as a friend of the court and appearance of counsel, in the appeal from the Lemlay decision in the Little Rock case.

6. The President of the United States should direct the Department of Justice to act now to protect the right of citizens to register and vote. In the nine months since the enactment of the 1957 Civil Rights Act, overt acts have been committed against prospective Negro registrants in some areas and numerous complaints have been submitted to the Department, but, to date, not a single case has reached a court of law. Unless immediate action is undertaken, thousands of Negro citizens will be denied the right to cast a ballot in the 1958 elections.

7. The President should direct the Department of Justice to act under existing statutes in the wave of bombings of churches, synagogues, homes, and community centers; also in the murderous brutality directed against Negro citizens in Dawson, Georgia, and other communities.

8. In order to counteract the deliberate hamstringing of the new Civil Rights Commission, the President should recommend to the Congress the extension of its life for at least a full year beyond its present expiration date.

9. The President should make it clear both in statement and in act that he believes in the principle that federal money should not be used to underwrite segregation in violation of the federal constitutional rights of millions of Negro citizens; and that this principle should be applied whether in matters of federal aid to education, hospitals, housing, or any other grants-in-aid to state and local governments. In support of national policy, the Federal Government should finance continuation of public schools where state funds are withdrawn because of integration.

In addition to the enumerations above, Negro citizens are deeply concerned over the efforts to curb the appellate jurisdiction of the Supreme Court, particularly the restrictions proposed in H.R. 3, a bill, which is both anti-civil rights and anti-labor.

Widespread discrimination against Negroes in employment persists in industry, business, and government and has been underscored by the general rise in unemployment. The problem is highlighted by repeated failures of efforts to enact national fair employment legislation and by the demonstrated ineffectiveness of administrative directives.

The need continues for vigorous enforcement of the Federal policy of non-discrimination in government employment. The national government can set an example by removing the barriers which have limited the employment of Negro citizens in all U. S. installations abroad, including the foreign service.

These recommendations are made in the belief that tensions between citizens in our country, and the anxieties of citizens themselves, will be eased and eventually erased if a clear national policy and a program of implementation are established by the Chief Executive of the nation.

> A. Philip Randolph
> Lester B. Granger
> Reverend Martin Luther King
> Roy Wilkins

> June 23, 1958

In a footnote referring to the press conference which followed the meeting, Siciliano refers to a question directed to Roy Wilkins by Louis Lautier, the only Negro member of the National Press Club Association. Wilkins, tagged the most militant member of the conferees, handled himself well and did not detonate. He later sent the President an interesting and respectful letter, with a carbon copy to me. I feel this letter should also be carried in this report to make it complete.

> June 25, 1958

Dear Mr. President:

I wish to express to you my personal appreciation of your courtesy in receiving the delegation of which I was a member on June 23 and the attention you gave to our presentation of the views of Negro American citizens on the present situation in which they find themselves.

In view of the extreme pressure of world affairs affecting the welfare of our country and the peace of the world, it was generous of you to devote an extended interview to us.

While the disabilities under which they live loom large in the minds and hearts of millions of Negro families, they

are loyal Americans and realize that their problems, while
important, do not enjoy priority over the problems facing the
nation in its international relations.

They feel, however, as we attempted to indicate, that their
situation has an important relation to international policy and
that this and other aspects of their citizenship difficulties will
have your careful consideration, as well as such action as is
deemed appropriate and effective.

Respectfully yours,

Roy Wilkins,
Executive Secretary

RW:jl

Honorable Dwight D. Eisenhower
President of the United States
The White House
Washington, D. C.

bc: E. Frederic Morrow

Crisis seemed to impinge upon crisis. Friday, June 20th, 1958
marked the close of one of the most dramatic and traumatic
weeks in the Eisenhower Administration. For months the
House Subcommittee on Legislative Oversight had been con-
ducting an inquiry into the operation of federal agencies
and whether officials of these agencies had been subjected to
political pressure to influence their decisions. On June 10th,
committee investigators introduced records showing that over
a two-year period Bernard Goldfine, a New England industri-
alist, had paid hotel bills of around $2,000 for Sherman
Adams in Boston. Mr. Goldfine had several cases before the
Federal Trade Commission and the Securities and Exchange
Commission. This information dropped on Washington like
hot lava from a volcano and spread across the world like a
prairie fire! The situation was incredible and incredulous.
To the politically wise and especially to the Democrats,
Sherman Adams for all his toughness and experience had
apparently made a colossal political blunder.

On June 12, Adams sent a letter to Representative Oren Harris of Arkansas, Chairman of the Subcommittee. The Governor said, in part:

Since this committee has chosen to make public the extent of the entertaining of myself and my family, on the part of an old friend, Mr. Goldfine, and has insinuated that because of this entertaining or friendship, Mr. Goldfine has received, on my intercession, favored treatment from the federal agencies, I feel that I should set the record straight. I categorically deny such insinuations. They are unwarranted and unfair.

He went on to explain that he and Mrs. Adams had known the Goldfines for more than fifteen years and that each had been entertained in the other's home. It was a close personal relationship. Mr. Goldfine had told the Governor that whenever he had the chance to come to Boston, he hoped that he would stay in Mr. Goldfine's suite at the Sheraton Plaza where he maintained an apartment. Whenever Mr. Adams had been in Boston, he accepted this offer.

He admitted that he had called the Federal Trade Commission once or twice to secure what he felt to be routine information for Mr. Goldfine. Adams felt that this information was the kind that any citizen could get from any federal agency merely for the asking. He had done the same thing in relation to the Securities and Exchange Commission. When he received the information, Adams did nothing further in the SEC case. He passed the FTC information on to Goldfine.

Among other charges the subcommittee was studying were that Goldfine gave the Governor a $2,400 Oriental rug and other expensive furnishings for his home, a $700 vicuna coat, and other presents.

On June 17, Sherman Adams requested an opportunity to testify before the subcommittee and his request was granted. He was subjected to pitiless questioning for two and a half hours. He testified that he may have acted a little imprudently in making phone call inquiries to the FTC and the SEC for his friend, but insisted that this was mere routine and the same services he and the White House staff performed in connection with many such requests. "I have no excuses to offer. I did not come here to make apologies to you or to the committee," Adams told Chairman Harris. "I do not wish to testify that I am a fledgling in this business of politics." But then he added, "If I had the decision now before me to make, I believe I would have acted a little more prudently."

He said that there had been no strings attached to the exchange of friendship with Goldfine. His home in Washington does have a $2,400 Oriental rug, as has been rumored, but it is only on loan from Goldfine to remedy the "shabbiness" Goldfine found in the rug they had had previously. He also admitted that his friend had adorned his home with two other small rugs.

Goldfine did give him a vicuna coat and had it tailored for him—but the actual skins cost Goldfine's mill $69.00—nowhere near the rumored price of $700. Mr. Adams said that his friend was proud of his mills and their products, and also had garments made up for Mrs. Adams and himself, just as he had done for each of the governors of states and territories in 1955.

Sherman Adams insisted that Bernard Goldfine had not benefited in any way in his relations with any branch of the federal government because he was a friend of Adams, and by the same token, Adams did not secure any favors or benefits for Goldfine.

This was a remarkable performance of courage and forbearance, but it did not stem the tide. Instead, from every corner of the nation and particularly from the Congress, came bitter denunciations of Adams and demands that he resign or be fired by the President immediately. Perhaps the most disheartening aspect of the whole event was the fact that so many Republican Congressmen and Senators joined with the angry pack snapping at his heels. Senators Edward Thye of Minnesota, William Knowland of California, Charles Potter of Michigan, and Barry Goldwater of Arizona (all Republicans and all up for re-election) demanded the Governor's scalp. The pressures upon the President to fire the Governor were tremendous. Everyone waited to see what the President would say about the matter at his Wednesday press conference.

I squeezed into the conference behind the President's Secret

Service bodyguards, because I realized that this was an important occasion. The room was crowded to the eaves. The President began by reading a statement so there would be no misunderstanding or misquotations. He said, in part:

> Anyone who knows Sherman Adams has never had any doubt of his personal integrity and honesty; no one has believed that he could be bought. But there is a feeling or belief that he was not sufficiently alert in making certain that the gifts of which he was the recipient could be so misinterpreted as to be considered attempts to influence his official actions. To that extent he has been, as he stated yesterday, "imprudent."
>
> The utmost prudence must necessarily be observed by everyone attached to the White House, because of the possible effect of any slightest inquiry, suggestion, or observation emanating from this office and reaching any other part of the Government. Carelessness must be avoided.
>
> My own conclusions on the entire episode are as follows: (1) I believe that the presentation made by Governor Adams to the Congressional Committee yesterday truthfully represents the pertinent facts; (2) I personally like Governor Adams; (3) I admire his abilities; (4) I respect him because of his personal and official integrity; (5) I need him.
>
> Admitting the lack of that careful prudence in this incident that Governor Adams yesterday referred to, I believe with my whole heart that he is an invaluable public servant, doing a difficult job efficiently, honestly, and tirelessly.
>
> Ladies and gentlemen, so far as I am concerned, this is all that I can, all that I shall, say.

This honest assertion by the President merely added more fuel to the flames. The cry was even greater than it had been at any time during the week—Adams must go!

This was a shocking series of events for all of us who met Sherman Adams at the same time the President did—back in 1952—and had been a part of the team ever since. It was a tragic thing to sit and watch Adams grow thinner and sadder day by day. One wanted to go up and tell him to have heart and to hold on, but it was difficult to do this to a man who for so long had had the reputation and demeanor of an iceberg.

The day after he returned from testifying on the Hill, he

came into the dining room with his wife and his friend Gerry Morgan. Despite the fact that he had given an admirable performance before the committee, he appeared blanched, tired, and sad. I went back to my office that afternoon and wrote him a little note, telling him of the homely philosophy of my grandfather who had fought his way out of slavery to become a free man and a foremost citizen. The essence of his philosophy had been that no matter how tough things got, "one must keep on keeping on." I also telephoned Mrs. Adams to tell her that my wife and I were with them in spirit and prayer.

The next day the Governor sent me a very cordial note of thanks for my personal support and faith in him. It is one I treasure.

One of the enigmas of my relationship with the White House had been the mystery of why I had not been given the position promised me at the beginning of the President's term in 1953, and why there was a two-year delay before a place was found for me on the White House staff. I was determined that before Sherman Adams left the White House, I would find out.

I had recently sent Adams a memorandum requesting a salary raise. My duties and responsibilities had widened and for the past two years I had to entertain visiting dignitaries at the request of the State Department or others. Also, I was being asked to speak to many more groups across the nation and often the fee available did not cover my actual expenses. Before I married I used my own funds to cover the deficits, but that was no longer possible.

Governor Adams had a reputation for not paying high salaries, and for never increasing those already in existence. He was adamant in the New England conviction that one should live within his salary no matter what. He had asked Andy Goodpaster to explore the contents of my memo, so Andy and I met twice to discuss it. A week later Governor Adams asked both of us to his office to give me a firm but gentle lecture on my financial condition.

I had to point out to the Governor that those demands on my salary were not of my desire nor making, but were a part of my official duties and the requirements of my position. I then laid the matter right on the line. I had exhausted my life's savings trying to protect my home and my mother's health before I came to Washington, and this situation obtained because the White House reneged on my employment after advising me to resign my job at CBS for immediate assignment in Washington. For over a year I had had to try to make enough money to live on and support my family but had never been able to recover from that unexpected event.

It was evident to me that this matter had preyed upon Adams's mind and that he felt he owed me some kind of explanation. He was his usual clear, frank, and honest self. He remembered clearly the promise that had been given me. It had not materialized at that time because no one had had any clear-cut idea of his own job and *certainly none as to what I could do that would not result in unfavorable comment*. He recalled discussing me with the "top people" and telling them that I was coming to Washington and to the White House, and their asking him, "But what will he do?" Governor Adams said there had been no answer to that question and that the decision at the time had been that *something would have to be worked out* so that my position would be more than just a sinecure. He said, "I hope you understand."

Yes, I understood very clearly. The reactionary forces on "The Team" had rebelled and no missionary was going to speak up and rock the fragile boat of the new administration. I could even accept this fact with equanimity. What made my anger erupt through the years was the fact no one in the White House had the courage or courtesy to call or write or tell me honestly what had happened. All of these people knew me and what I stood for and they should have realized they could be frank and to the point with me.

A high-ranking administration figure had told me a year or two before the governor's meeting that General Persons had taken umbrage at my proposed appointment and had indicated to colleagues that he would walk out of the White House taking the white secretaries with him if I appeared. This was southern chivalry at its best and I regret I was denied the privilege of helping in its execution.

Whatever the true story, during my tenure I received only

Governor Adams's official version and for the rest of my life can only conjecture about the untold part.

However, this was the first meeting I had had with Governor Adams since his involvement in the hideous Goldfine matter. He looked better than he had looked for weeks and he was thinking clearly and talking with assurance and conviction. He gave me the salary raise and at the end of the conference stood up and gave me a particularly firm handshake and we looked each other straight in the eye as we had always done.

Chapter Twenty-eight

It is interesting and significant the way Vice President Nixon moved in and out of my life, not only during White House days, but even later. We established a very fine rapport on our African trip in 1957 and after that we seemed to mesh without discord or trouble.

In the White House I was ever aware of the fragility of tenure on the presidential staff or in cabinet jobs. The letters, or Certificates of Appointment, always bear the ominous phrase ". . . to serve at the will of the President . . ." Hence I was always trying to develop plans to handle any contingency—present or future.

Late in July, 1958 I went up to Capitol Hill to see the Vice President on personal business. I wanted to talk to him about my dilemma of whether I should attempt to make a career out of government—or go ahead with my present plans to try to go into business at the end of the current administration. This seemed to be a good time to be thinking about the future. Already several top aides had resigned and returned to business while they were still on top.

I asked the Vice President whether he thought my pioneering efforts in government had borne fruit and if he felt that there might be a place for me with my talents in any future administration. I told him I had come to him as a personal friend and not because he was Vice President and I wanted his candid opinion and advice.

He stretched his long frame out from his chair and gazed intently ahead for a few seconds. He then turned to me directly and said:

> You are not only a rare Negro, but a rare human being with qualities that are very valuable to your Government. You must continue to break through into the new areas, achieve goals, and help blaze a trail that will make it easier to integrate other Negroes into top government echelons. One of your greatest assets, Fred, is the fact that you do not resent being a Negro, and you do not use your color as an excuse for any misfortune you may encounter.

He warmed up to the subject as he went along and you could almost see the wheels turning in his head as he expounded further on his whole attitude toward the status of Negroes in the Federal Government.

He was critical of naming Blacks to positions that dealt with race relations or "minority matters." He admitted that his attitude and view differed from many in public life and even from the present administration! He pointed out that despite the fact that Val Washington was doing an exceptional job at the Republican National Committee, it was a mistake to have a Black in that spot because not only would he or she be emotionally involved in any problem concerning races, but that it was rather pathetic to see a minority person laboring on something that consistently pointed up race or color.

The Vice President was super-critical of the position that Max Rabb had held in the White House as minority advisor to the President. He felt that this merely made it possible for prejudiced persons to feel that Max's job consisted of looking out for the welfare of Jews or Blacks and trying to make it possible for them to reach places of influence in Government. If anyone had to be placed in those spots, it should be someone who was not a member of a minority, and if the position had to deal with matters of race, its occupant should not be a Negro. He said that he was in favor of qualified Blacks being designated as ambassadors, but believed that they should not be sent only to all-Black countries.

I thoroughly enjoyed this revealing session with Vice President Nixon and was pleased that he was thinking in such a progressive vein. Before I departed he said;

> If I ever achieve any other position in Government, I will
> utilize it to permit Negroes greater opportunities to serve their
> country in positions of prestige and influence.

This was really a gallant and bold statement. It was a signal to me that the Vice President was planning for 1960 and he was certain to be the Republican candidate to succeed President Eisenhower.

As I look back upon this hour twenty-one years later, I can recall how impressed I was by this man Nixon's keenness of mind, deep perception of a centuries-old problem, and his apparent sincerity of purpose to forge ahead and make progress in a long-ignored area of national responsibility. However, as our relationship ripened through the years, I was distressed as the Republican party's reactionary attitude towards minorities apparently seeped into Nixon's political bloodstream.

In early September, 1958 after the Supreme Court heard the final arguments on the Little Rock case, I appealed for a meeting of high Administration leaders to discuss a strategy to stem the loud cries from the nation of ". . . a leaderless country." I had requested this meeting after receiving a letter from Roy Wilkins describing the bitterness among Blacks in the nation "because of the recent arrest of Martin Luther King by Montgomery, Alabama policemen, his subhuman treatment, and the general feeling on the part of Negroes that they were being ignored by the leaders of their government and would have to go it alone."

The meeting was held in the office of Gerry Morgan, Counsel to the President, and included Assistant Attorney General Wilson White, in charge of the Civil Rights Division of the Justice Department, Gordan Tiffany, Executive Director of the Commission on Civil Rights, Bryce Harlow, Presidential Assistant, and Rocco Siciliano.

We discussed what the President's role ought to be in this present raging controversy.

Bryce Harlow reporting on a recent trip through certain sections of the South and Southwest, said that the feeling in those areas was that the President was not showing leadership or initiative in this crisis and that the country was slowly drifting toward chaos and confusion over the bitter school controversy.

Bryce felt that there were certain forces for good in the country that, given leadership, direction, and encouragement, would mold sentiment into carrying out the Supreme Court's original decision.

The group felt that no matter what the President's personal views, there was a clear mandate for him to take the initiative to encourage citizenry to put their personal feelings behind them and try to make this facet of our democracy work. We believed that the President should—at the earliest possible moment after the Supreme Court handed down its decision in the present case—go to the country on television and radio to stress the moral necessity of obeying the court's decision.

I was pleased at this unanimity of opinion. It took real courage for staff members to tell the President their true feelings. The situation was distasteful and all of us would have liked to avoid it—but each was aware of his responsibility to the President and the country.

After the meeting we called the attorney general and told him our feelings. He advised us to prepare the text for a possible speech for the President. Judge William White of the Department of Justice and I were appointed to develop the text. We did. The President never used it. Later in his State of the Union Address in January, 1959, he indicated he would use whatever powers were necessary to carry out the provisions of the Constitution.

On September 22, 1958, Sherman Adams announced, in a dramatic radio-television speech, that he had resigned as Assistant to the President.

"I have done no wrong," he said.

David Lawrence, Columnist of the *New York Herald Tribune*, brilliantly and succinctly expressed my views on what happened to Sherman Adams. In his column of September 23rd he wrote:

An innocent man went to the gallows of American politics tonight—convicted not by a jury of his peers, but by the political hangmen of the hour. His head was not bowed in shame, for his conscience was clear. He yielded only to the law of expediency, which enforces its criminal verdict to satisfy the passion of the mob, even in politics . . .

My diary account of September 23, 1958 states the following:

"Governor Adams's address to the nation was a masterly, solemn, dignified performance, and at the close of his eight-minute talk, his voice appeared to break and he seemed on the verge of tears. As Catherine and I watched the performance we were extremely touched. Sherman Adams meant more to me, perhaps, than any other member of the White House staff, with the exception of the President.

Since I first met him on the campaign train in 1952, he has taken a distinct interest in my career and welfare and he has never hesitated to help me wherever and whenever he could.

There was a camaraderie between us that is hard to define. *It was he* who brought me into the White House after two years' delay while a "climate" was being fashioned for my entry. His door was always open to me, and his remarkable wife, Rachel, has been my wife's friend and protector. No matter where we met her or under what circumstances, she always made certain that we felt welcomed and relaxed.

It will be impossible to fill his place. Perhaps it is true that no human being is indispensable, but Sherman Adams comes pretty near to filling the role in this present situation. Perhaps the President is the only living man who knows what Adams has shouldered and what he has done in helping to carry the burdens of the President's office. Only those of us who worked with him knew of his selflessness, dedication, fierce loyalty to his country, and incomparable integrity."

As Sherman Adams prepared to leave, there was a barren atmosphere in his old office and a deep melancholia among those of us who had been close to him, both officially and personally.

I congratulated General Wilton Persons upon his appointment to the old Adams post, and received a friendly reply from him. I knew that Persons would try to do a good job because of his absolute dedication to the President. I knew, however, that from this point on, it would be difficult to get through to the President any suggestions or counsel in the matter of racial problems and particularly in the delicate field of civil rights and desegregation.

Adams had supported me solidly in my activities, my thinking, and my efforts to make both the President and his administration look good in the eyes of Black Americans. But now, people in the Administration who recognized my bond with Adams realized that I was more or less alone as far as having a strong friend at court, and already the signs were there that all would not go well in the days ahead.

Chapter Twenty-nine

The defeat of the Republican Party candidates in the country-wide elections of November 1958 was devastating! I was glad that it was a crushing defeat because I hoped it would indicate to even the most obtuse that something would have to be done organically to restructure the party from top to bottom if it were to survive.

Every place I spoke during the campaign the atmosphere was heavy with defeat. In every place there was an indication that the leadership was archaic, misinformed, and still holding onto blueprints of the dead past. All over the country it appeared to me that people were not voting against the Republicans so much as they were voting for a hope that new faces and a new party would give leadership in the present perilous times.

Blacks had a large hand in the Democratic victory. Their role indicated that besides civil rights, they were interested in economics first and foremost, and through union activities, they were being taught that the Democratic Party offered them greater hope for job opportunities and for participation in party politics at a local level.

A few days after the election I drew up a memo for the top leadership of the Republican party. I pointed out that in the key cities in the country where Blacks held the balance of power, the Republicans had made little or no effort to interest them, to give them an opportunity to participate in party councils, or to become an integral part of day-to-day activities.

In most areas where I had been, the Republican leadership was aloof and still looked upon Blacks as a lower class and talked down to them rather than gave them any chance for equality. I stated flatly that unless the Republican party could come up with a new format in a very short time, it was doomed to defeat and failure in 1960.

After Governor Adams's departure, the White House machine stalled almost completely. There was an atmosphere of indecision and fear which seemed to affect the attitude and morale of the entire staff. It is difficult to describe or estimate the position that Adams held and the myriad things he did. He played an active part in nearly every decision made in the White House for the first six years, and he took the brunt of almost every fight and skirmish, no matter whom it might be with. He never shirked a duty or put off making a difficult decision. When all hell broke loose because of some White House decision, Adams, without debate or self-pity, would take the responsibility for the decision.

In all fairness, it was easy to understand how a new person would find it difficult to step into his shoes. His many responsibilities had been divided among several persons after his departure and this made it difficult to get a quick, clean-cut decision on anything. There was vacillation, indecision, and lack of leadership. No one wanted to accept the responsibility for making tough decisions; consequently matters piled up that should have been decided weeks before.

A few days after he took over Governor Adams's title as "Assistant to the President," General Persons called me on the telephone and asked me if I'd do him the courtesy of coming to his office for a talk. He greeted me with a warm handshake upon arrival and said:

"Fred, I have a tough job to do now; I need all the help I can get. I just want to ask you to do me a favor. If you have any more 'Little Rock' problems, or whatever, don't come to me with them. Go to anybody else."

He continued: "This damn civil rights Black business has broken up my family! And my family can't understand how I can serve a yankee President anyhow; and then when I've got your situation on top of it, it's a little more than I can abide! Now, you're my friend, and, just don't ever come to me with any Black problems . . ."

"I promise you, General, I won't," I replied.

Let it be said that General Persons, despite his emotional reactions to Black-white relations, was basically a gentleman. He respected me in my position, and after I got to the White House, I don't know that he ever did anything spiteful to keep me from remaining there. Because I knew his feelings and he knew mine, we were able to make it.

He had vehemently opposed my employment but after being exposed to me for a few years we became "guarded friends." I found him a very estimable gentleman, and I was never aware that he turned his powerful influence against me as a person. Against my ideas, perhaps; but he respected my integrity.

I made a speech in Detroit on March 25, 1959, before the Wayne County Republican Club. Michigan Republicans had been steadily losing elections since 1950, and at long last the reasons seemed to concern the Republican leaders in that area deeply.

On the way from the airport, one of the party officials asked me bluntly: "What do we have to do to make friends with Black voters and get their support?" This made me extremely angry, but fortunately I restrained myself and tried to give a measured answer. This question, however, gave me added ammunition for my speech before the club which had turned out in record numbers to hear me.

I took the gloves off and let them have it. The sum and substance of the whole address was that Blacks still stood on the fringe of party activity and until given a full-fledged part in party councils and office-holding, the party could not count on their allegiance. It seemed incredible to me in a city like Detroit with its melting-pot millions that party leaders did not know the answer to this question.

In almost any city the Black seldom sees top leaders; thus, desires and wants must be made known through some straw-boss. Governor G. Mennon Williams of Michigan and the state Democratic Party had gone out of their way to make friends of Black voters. Not only that, but the governor made some outstanding appointments of Blacks to positions of substance and stature, and this was a record that the Republicans could not match.

There were slight repercussions to this speech, but nothing to match those that came after my address before the Republican Women's Convention held in Washington on April 14th. Here again, I used the Michigan situation for my theme and a little more sharply tried to bring home the fact that Republicans could not expect Blacks to be extremely grateful for what Lincoln had done since it was merely returning to them their God-given rights of freedom and personal dignity.

Blacks facing the reality of the times were deeply interested in economics as well as civil rights. They were affected by the ebb and flow of national life like any others; and until Republicans stopped trying to devise special methods of dealing with Black citizens, they would repel rather than attract them to the Republican banner. It was true that Republicans had done more in the last hundred years on the matter of civil rights than any other political party. It was likewise true that the Democrats—particularly the southern wing—had merely given lip service to those ideals, and that the southern wing was intolerant toward any kind of progress in this area. However, the Democrats did a better job of political public relations. Even though Democrats were just as insincere as the Republicans, they appeared to give Blacks opportunities to participate in party councils; and, through activity in labor unions and grass-roots politics, helped them find more job opportunities than the Republicans.

I had hardly finished my speech before all hell broke loose.

Even though the audience had given me a standing ovation, it was evident that the leadership on the platform was pretty sore about the whole matter. Officials soon started calling the White House to brand me a traitor, an ingrate, and many other uncomplimentary names. No press coverage of the speech had been intended but, ironically enough, the Associated Press rushed in, grabbed the speech, put it on its wires, and sent it around the world.

The President was in Augusta, but officials of the National Republican Committee made known their displeasure to some of the White House staff. I was asked to interpret certain accusations in my speech in the hope that they did not mean what they said. However, they meant exactly what they said, so I was not able to heal any wounds by further interpretations.

The response from the Black community was tremendous! Telegrams, letters, and telephone calls came from both Democrats and Republicans. The feeling was that this was the first time in the memory of living man that any Black jobholder with a position on my level had dared to stand up while occupying that position and tell off the party that had given him the job.

This was no smart-alecky stunt on my part. My conscience had been whipping me for many months as I repeatedly glimpsed the complete indifference of Republican leadership in cities, counties, and states, and within national administration to Black participation in party life. In the beginning, the Eisenhower Administration had appointed a few to prominent positions, but this stopped after a dozen or more had been appointed; and, as they resigned, were promoted, or died, there had not been Black successors in these positions or in comparable positions. This meant, then, that Blacks had lost ground and, by the same token, during the past four years the Democrats had gained ground tremendously. It was safe to say that approximately 75% of Blacks who voted, voted for Democratic candidates.

I did not know whether what I had done would do any good, because Republicans were reluctant to see the handwriting on the wall in this area. But I had carried out my duty to my party and the Administration; and no matter what the consequences were for me, it was a tremendous relief to have expressed my convictions.

An interesting event during the summer of 1959 was the outdoor supper party held by the President on his farm at Gettysburg in June. He had held a similar affair back in 1955 when most of the staff members had been invited. This particular occasion afforded the same opportunity to those who had joined the staff since the first party in 1955. It was a completely cosmopolitan and democratic event, because it included not only executive members of the staff, but also the household staff including maids, cooks, butlers, the White House police, and the Secret Service men and their families.

It was a gorgeous afternoon to drive to Gettysburg and the President's farm and his beautiful home were something to behold. I was happy to discover that this comfortable place offered rest and peace and satisfaction to this great man who had given so much to his country, and it was my solemn hope that he would have many happy years to spend there after his retirement from the Presidency. The Eisenhowers were gracious hosts and they gave much of their time and attention to the party.

Again, this affair brought home to Catherine and me the fact that some of our executive staff members and their wives were completely insecure socially and made themselves ridiculous by their conduct on these occasions, as they suddenly tried to avoid us. This was sharply evident at the garden party because Mrs. Eisenhower was so gracious, kind, and thoughtful and spent a generous portion of her time talking to us, telling us little personal features of the farm.

There were at least 300 persons at the party and as we walked about the spacious grounds bumping into this person and that, we were amused when some of my colleagues would beat a hasty retreat in the opposite direction as soon as they spied us. It was the old story of the secure ones seeking us out for conversation, suggesting that maybe we would like to join them in doing this or that or the other thing. After the secure ones had done this, very often the insecure ones would pretend that this was the first time they had seen us and it was so nice that we had come. After many years of such treatment we were learning to meet this kind of conduct with an unemotional mien and we resolved to let the others stew in their juice.

Another event of great satisfaction to me during this period was the President's nomination of my brother, Dr. John H. Morrow, to be Ambassador to the Republic of Guinea. Neither John nor I had sought this appointment for him; apparently it was one that had been decided upon by the State Department solely because of John's extraordinary ability as a French scholar, his knowledge of the area where he would work, and his personal friendship with many of the people from Guinea, whom he had met during his stay at the Sorbonne and subsequent trips in France.

The Washington Post editorially raised the question as to whether or not a scholar was the best person to send to such a difficult post since the Russians had made such tremendous inroads during the short span of that country's independence. The *Post* also dragged the racial question into the situation by suggesting that the naming of a Black as diplomat to an African country was presumptuous and condescending.

What the *Post* had forgotten or ignored was the fact that whites had lost face in Africa and, because of the previous policies of white countries, it was possible that Africans were willing to deal more freely with a Black representative than they might with a white. Another factor was that ability should have been the overriding consideration in any of these appointments and color merely incidental. Some of the southern newspapers gave John's nomination complete endorsement and it was with a deep sense of pride that they pointed out that "one of our boys made it." He was at that time head of the Department of Foreign Languages at North Carolina College.

The Cameroon in West Africa became independent on January 1, 1960. A few days later President William V.S. Tubman was to be sworn in again as President of Liberia. An American delegation was to be sent to both celebrations and I had been named to the official delegation which was to be headed by Ambassador Lodge of the United Nations.

In preliminary discussions with the White House and the State Department, I was told that my wife could go along with the delegation, particularly in view of the fact that an Air Force plane would be used for transportation. In the event that commercial airlines had to be used, the wives would not accompany the delegation.

About six days before the trip was scheduled to begin, I had still heard nothing from the State Department as to what would be required in the way of dress; nor had I been advised as to when briefings about the trip would be held. I called the State Department for information. I was shocked when I was told that my wife could not accompany me on the trip because "all the spaces on the plane had been spoken for." This amazed me and I could not understand how "all the spaces had been spoken for" when I was a member of the delegation with all the same prerogatives that anyone else would have. The spokesman informed me that only the wives of certain members of the delegation had space on the plane. Ironically enough, these were the wives of the white men of the delegation. None of the Black men of the delegation would be permitted to take their wives.

This was an incredible situation. It was difficult for me to believe that the State Department could have itself bullied into this untenable position. Here the United States was sending a delegation to a Black country with only the white members of the delegation permitted the privilege of bringing their wives. It was even more astounding in view of the fact that I was a close personal friend of the President of Liberia and that the Liberian Government had even offered me transportation for this very occasion. I could not accept such transportation, of course, in view of constitutional limitations. Furthermore, an American company doing extensive business in Liberia was so anxious for my wife and me to go that they also put space on their plane at our disposal. This we also had to turn down.

The State Department was so sticky about the situation and I was so incensed that I told them to remove my name from the delegation and I did not go.

This incident caused a great deal of furor in the Black press and in certain circles and I was deluged with phone calls for information. I refused to comment on this at all, but newspaper accounts were so accurate and clear that the story was well known throughout the country.

This situation highly distressed the officials of the Liberian Government. The State Department made no effort to apologize to me or to offer any explanation beyond the fact that there were sleeping accommodations only for a limited number. My contention all along had been: either all wives or none. There could never be a plausible explanation as to why the wives of only white officials were included while the wives of Black officials were not. This kind of bungling made whites persona non grata in certain parts of Africa and Asia, and the tragedy of it is that our State Department never seems to learn a lesson from its "booboos."

One day early in January, 1960, I was summoned to General Persons's office for a personal conference. This was unusual because in the course of carrying out my responsibilities, I had seldom come into contact with the General. I knew that this conference would be important since he had requested that I come over as soon as possible.

Long ago I had learned to respect this southern gentleman. I could appreciate all the emotions he experienced when we were forced together either on social or even business occasions. However, through the years he had learned to adapt himself admirably to whatever was happening and we enjoyed the best possible cordial relationship. There were times when he seemed to me quite self-conscious, but this was understandable.

When I sat down in the General's office, he immediately got to the subject at hand in his characteristic fashion. He said it was not his policy ever to prevent anyone on the staff from seeking new opportunities for advancement or other employment; but in the case at hand he had been forced to interfere and he wanted me to know about it.

Persons said that the Nixon group had approached him a few weeks ago and had asked him to release me so that I could work for the Vice President, apparently on his pre-convention campaign. The general said that the Nixon forces were prepared to offer me a very responsible position. He said, however, that he had discouraged them. He said that I was one of the President's top staff and if I left at this time, it would give the wrong impression to the public and the press, and merely serve as an opportunity for writers and other speculators to have a field day.

Persons also felt that at this early stage of the game, it would be unwise to expose my hand as to what I would do in the coming election. He emphasized that to get too far out in front before a candidate is chosen is to leave one's self wide open for attack and abuse. He felt that it would be wise for me to remain on the staff at least until a candidate was chosen and then leave very quietly if such were my desire.

The general realized, of course, that he had usurped my prerogative to make decisions and said that I was free to do whatever I wished. He was merely trying to give me fatherly advice, and, very frankly, he had no desire for the President's team to be broken up at this time.

The fact that the Nixon forces wanted me was news to me. From various sources from time to time had come questions as to my attitude toward the Vice President, but there had been no specific offer. This one seemed pretty definite since the President's chief assistant had been sounded out.

I assured the General that I had no immediate intention of leaving the President's staff; I was completely dedicated to the President and would be eternally grateful to him for the exceptional opportunity he had given me to serve on his staff.

It would mean sacrifice to remain because this was the propitious time for staff members to leave. Our worth would diminish as the term grew shorter and many were already cashing in on their present affiliation with the President. I chose to stay on until the situation became clearer and I was able to give the idea more thought and planning.

Chapter Thirty

The catastrophic defeat suffered by the Republicans in the November, 1960 Presidential election resulted from incredible ineptness. Somewhere in the highest echelon of the Party decisions had been made that foredoomed the Republican team to defeat. It is true that the Nixon-Kennedy debates represented a sad mistake for the Nixon managers to make. Nixon was Vice President of the United States, universally known, and with a legendary reputation for sound and logical debate. Kennedy was practically unknown and had everything to gain by engaging Nixon in public debate. Nixon had nothing to gain—but a great deal to lose.

However, this wasn't the key blunder. The keystone of the defeat was the indefensible decision to ignore the Black vote and go hell-bent for the coy but predictable South. Even without the benefit of polls or knowledgeable Black advice, even the dullest politician should have known that Black voters held the balance of power in the pivotal and border states of the nation. These states had to be carried by any candidate who wished to win. Blacks, spurred on by the NAACP, labor, and other liberal organizations, had registered in unprecedented numbers and were determined to play a vital role in the 1960 election. They stood in the wings just waiting to be wooed and won by candidates who understood their need and deep interest in the matter of first-class citizenship. Despite the issue of Kennedy's religion, this was the easiest campaign of all.

As early as January, 1959, the Black mood was very clear to me. I started early in the year petitioning the Republican high command to organize its activities locally and nationally to attract the Black vote. I sent countless notes to Leonard Hall, the national Republican Chairman; Senator Thruston Morton, former Chairman; and to staff members in Mr. Nixon's office, outlining what must be done if we were to hold what we had and gain more. Often the notes were ignored or the replies innocuous. It was maddening!

I was in the "doghouse" with the high command for my address at the National Republican Women's Club meeting. In some areas, like Washington, D.C. where I made the speech, no Black woman could join the Republican Women's Club. Blacks were relegated to Jim-Crow organizations and Jim-Crow activity. In my speech, I predicted the debacle of November, 1960 unless the party mended its ways assuring Blacks of equality of participation.

The administration was tired and at this point was fighting a holding action, so nothing officially was done about firing me. From time to time during the early part of 1960 a few interested staff members in the White House talked informally about the coming convention and election. Bob Merriam of the White House staff became the liaison person between the committee and the administration. He helped work on the composition of convention delegates, program, and strategy. It was largely through his help and intervention that I got slight Black representation on the convention program. They gave me a three-minute spot on the Salute-to-Eisenhower Night and selected Mrs. Jewel Rogers of Chicago to second the nomination of the vice presidential candidate.

Vice President Nixon's acceptance speech at the Chicago convention was a masterpiece, delivered with conviction and courage. He took charge in a manner that befitted a fighting candidate and it gave heart to the flagging spirits of many apprehensive Republicans. In retrospect, I believe that Mr. Nixon reached the high point of the campaign and perhaps of his career with his acceptance speech at the 1960 convention. Never again did he reach such heights of conviction, sincerity, determination, and boldness. His appearance, attitude, and self-determination were the epitome of dynamic leadership. It was a deliriously happy audience that saluted this inspired leader.

One of the unsolved mysteries of the 1960 campaign is: whatever happened to the Nixon that was first unveiled to the nation in Chicago in July? Never again during the campaign did he approach this high rise of compelling leadership; never again did his followers thrill as they did that hot July night when he took over the reins of the Republican Party.

As far as the convention was concerned, the campaign got off to a good start as regards concern for the Black vote. Nixon personally invited me to the secret midnight caucus of the "party greats" to pick the vice presidential candidate. It was the first time in history that a Black had participated actively in such proceedings. Some of the participants seemed concerned when a Secret Service man escorted me into the heavily guarded room but the Vice President quickly assured them that I had been invited on the same basis as any of them.

It was a historic meeting. Some of the hopefuls like Mitchell, Secretary of Labor, and Seaton, Secretary of the Interior, were present. However, no holds were barred and each when called upon, spoke his piece. I was among the first to be asked by the Vice President, who presided, who my choice was and why. I picked Henry Cabot Lodge because "not even the NAACP can be against his superb liberal record."

The meeting went on far into the early morning because all the "wheels" had to speak ad infinitum. In the end the final decision was Lodge. It was obvious that he was wanted by Nixon and perhaps that is who it would have been even if a majority had thought otherwise. It occurred to me that if

Nixon had me in this vital spot, he intended to use me in a similar spot in the campaign and this I wanted very much.

I had flown to the convention with President Eisenhower in his new jet plane. I had gone up to his vacation retreat in Newport the day before to be on hand for an early morning departure. I had landed in Newport in early afternoon and was invited to sail on the Presidential yacht. It was a delightful interlude and one of the most pleasant evenings I have spent with the White House brass. They were relaxed and friendly during the two-hour sail.

We flew into Chicago at noon the next day to a tumultuous welcome. We landed at O'Hare, helicoptered to a small field in midtown, then motored at a snail's pace through a million spectators who lined the streets all the way to the hotel.

The night of the "Salute to Eisenhower" was a trying one for me. I was originally allotted five minutes for my television speech. Then a disinterested and officious character managing proceedings cut me to two minutes. At the afternoon rehearsal I did not get a chance to "try out," and only with tenacious insistence did my speech get put on a teleprompter. When I arrived at the convention that night I could not get in because I had not been provided with the correct pass and the guards would not recognize my White House pass. By sheer luck, fifteen minutes before I was to go on, I ran into a Secret Service man who got me in. I was a nervous wreck.

The opening line of my speech, which went around the world, said: "One hundred years ago today, my grandfather was a slave. Tonight I stand before you a trusted assistant of the President of the United States!" The applause was deafening!

The President had arrived early enough to hear part of the program and was seated off stage in the VIP lounge watching proceedings on television. He was furious when the station to which he was tuned cut me out for a commercial and chit-chat by the commentators. He expressed his anger about this incident vigorously later. These same commentators and this same network had cut out the Black speakers at the Democratic Convention in Los Angeles a week before. It hardly seemed like an accident.

I returned home willing, ready, and enthusiastic to participate in the campaign and to give my best efforts for the party
and for Richard Nixon. However, the call was a long time in
coming and the part given me to play was insulting. I took a
two months' leave of absence without pay from the White
House to work in the Nixon campaign. Since February
Leonard Hall, the party chairman, had promised me a prominent and vital place in the campaign hierarchy but it did not
materialize. Nixon's young campaign managers and staff had
different ideas and it became apparent to me at once that they
had more zeal than knowledge. The first person one met when
one went into the office off the elevator thought he knew more
about Blacks than any Black extant. Consequently, the campaign team never accepted or sought advice on this delicate
and vital subject.

During the entire two months in the campaign office I never
had a secretary or anyone to answer my considerable mail. I
never had a dime to spend for anything except personal expenses: no literature, no workers, and no assistants. It was a
tragic moment. Black leaders from all over the nation called
me day and night for financial help and literature and they
could not believe me when I reported that neither was available.

Val Washington, Director of Minorities at the national committee, was in a similar predicament. He had practically no
money and was trying to direct a nationwide campaign with
about five people. His pitiful pleas for help fell on deaf and
unsympathetic ears. The only national speaker of any importance we had on the road was Jackie Robinson, the famous
baseball star. He made a great personal sacrifice to help
Nixon, the man of his choice. Yet he, too, had a heavy and
broken heart over the ignorance with which the campaign was
conducted.

Late in the campaign I joined the Nixon entourage on the
road. Unlike the Eisenhower campaigns of 1952 and 1956, I
was never seen with the Vice President. I rode in caravans in a
rear car and was never called into parleys or strategy meetings.

In the closing days of the campaign, Reverend Martin
Luther King, Black idol and civil rights leader, was thrown
into jail in Atlanta on a trivial charge. It was an international

sensation. It was the moment for American leadership to speak. I begged the Nixon managers by memorandum and in person to have the Vice President make a statement deploring the situation under which King was jailed. They demurred. They thought it bad strategy. The next day I joined the Nixon campaign train in Illinois. I urged his press secretary to have him take some action. I even drafted a telegram for the Vice President to send to the Mayor of Atlanta. However, the press secretary put the draft in his pocket to "think about it."

Twenty-four hours later King had been freed from jail. His freedom came after the intercession of the Democratic Presidential candidate, John F. Kennedy. He had scored a ten-strike. Kennedy had not only wired the mayor of Atlanta in King's behalf and his brother Bobby had apparently talked to some other officials, but John Kennedy had phoned King's wife expressing his concern and asking if he could be of assistance. This act won the election! Kennedy's action electrified the Black community and tens of thousands of them went over to the Kennedy banner.

John Kennedy became President-elect of the United States. Many factors contributed to his election, which was close; but one incontrovertible fact was evident: he carried the crucial, essential Black vote. Although he was a babe in the woods as regards Blacks, Mr. Kennedy had keen, intelligent Black advisors and he obviously followed their advice. The results of the campaign contained many valuable lessons for Republican leaders and all politicians. First, the strategy to woo the solid South and ignore the available Black vote was a costly blunder. The South was still too emotional over slavery and Reconstruction to come over to the Republicans in a wholesale manner. Likewise, white people had to stop believing they "know the Black." For a long while in this country it would be well to ask some knowledgeable Black to assess objectively Black attitude and mood on a given subject. In Republican headquarters every person there was an expert.

THE REDISCOVERY OF RICHARD NIXON

Long after his defeat in the Presidential election of 1960, Richard Nixon continued to be part of my life. I did not see

Mr. Nixon again for almost ten years. After his defeat in California, when he ran for governor in 1962, he returned to New York to join a prestigious Wall Street law firm. His office was almost across the street from my own at the Bank of America, International.

After that I saw him occassionally and he invited me to his Fifth Avenue home for a talk when he became the Republican candidate for President in 1968. At that time he called his aide Dwight Chapin and told him to inform Leonard Garment that he wanted Fred Morrow to play a vital and important part in the campaign and to "set it up."

Mr. Garment was a brilliant attorney but a novice in politics. He was in charge of minority affairs and I recoiled when I saw the participants of the first meeting he invited me to. They were well-known dead beats, con men, and persons without influence or character who could only bring headaches and discredit to any candidate. So I informed Mr. Garment that I did not wish to participate and we agreed to disagree. Hence, I was not active in that campaign.

In my tour of duty at the White House, I traveled across the world with Mr. Nixon. I was always proud to be an American. I was always proud when it came time for him to respond to a toast or to make an observation in a foreign country because the man was able; he was brilliant at times, no question about it. He was an excellent Vice President. I think he got a little peeved on our trip to Africa when he found out that Nkrumah spent more time with me than he did with Nixon. When we got back to the White House and reported on the trip, his answer to a question was: "Why don't you ask Fred Morrow; he seems to know more about . . ."

When he was Vice President he gave no indication that he would end his political career in disgrace and shame. He was obviously a very ambitious man. His background had been very modest and you could feel the man trying to get away, trying to rise above his past. He did not want his family to experience any of his painful memories of the past.

I remember the rainy, snowy morning when we took off on the trip to Africa in March 1957. Mrs. Nixon was my seat mate. A wonderful, pleasant, affable woman, she was bursting with excitement and good humor when she sat down. "Fred," she exclaimed, "I'm so excited because yesterday Dick went out and bought our first home." Then she whispered, "What he used for money I don't know, but we've got a home!" Through the ensuing years Mrs. Nixon was a beautiful, warm, honest, down-to-earth friend. She always made Catherine and me feel welcome and happy to be in her presence. She was a great American asset.

When I abruptly left Mr. Nixon's campaign train in 1960 after I could not convince his staff of the importance of dealing with Coretta King and the Georgia officials, it was his advisors rather than Nixon who did me in.

I believe what was missing in the Nixon White House were a few persons with the guts to tell the President the bare truth on vital issues. It takes a lot of mettle to tell the President of the United States unpleasant news or to be objectively critical of his views. It takes super courage when the President has spun something he thinks may be feasible, and you mull it over a hundred times, see flaws in it, say, "Sir, I'm afraid that . . ."

James Hagerty, Eisenhower's press secretary, was a man of great courage and a perfect presidential assistant. He could, without blinking an eye, stand before the President and say, "Sir, I respectfully disagree with your proposal." I think that kind of man was missing in the Nixon administration. It appears that his youthful aides were so anxious to serve and do the President's bidding that this desire overrode any sense of morality or eternal good. They helped to hang their own leader.

I have long mused over President Nixon's fall from grace and high office. My reaction is one of extreme sorrow and regret. It is my considered judgment that if Mr. Nixon had been elected President on his first try in 1960, there would never have been a Watergate.

I feel I knew the Nixon of 1960. I had watched him charm and fascinate people around the world with his wisdom and astuteness. He was neither dumb nor gross. He was sharp, able, and knowledgeable. My theory is that he grew bitter and callous through the years by his recurring defeats and frustrations. His loss of the close presidential race to Senator John F. Kennedy must have left a gaping wound in his very soul. He lost because of an inept and second-rate staff. If only they had courted Mrs. King, the Black vote would have elected him. John Kennedy did and won by a whisker.

In the 1960 race Mr. Nixon wanted to win on his own. He ignored the veterans of the Eisenhower administration in favor of his friends who were untried on the big time and who failed in the big leagues when they couldn't fathom the pitcher. His campaign director was a nice social animal but a bust in his job. He couldn't perceive the depths and heights of a national campaign.

When Nixon was elected in 1968 he had much to vindicate. He had had eight years to develop a cancer of distrust and hate and a determination to "get even." As President, he would acquire for himself the purple robes of a king, emperor, and supreme being. He would destroy those little guys who had dared to delay him on his road to omnipotence nine years before!

AUT CAESAR AUT NULLUS! (Either a Caesar or a nobody!)

Chapter Thirty-one

If President Eisenhower had been more of a political animal and more tough-minded on the matter of civil rights and if he had been able to go the whole mile in the field of race relations, a great many of the country's problems in the 1960s would not have happened. I am talking about the riots, killings, burnings, and devastation in the Black uprisings—or, rather, rebellions—of the sixties.

I prophesied these inevitable disasters in countless memoranda to top White House staff beginning in 1955. Years after my departure members of the Administration meeting me somewhere in the world would state: "If we had only listened and acted. . . ."

American Blacks were set to love President Eisenhower. But when he failed to come to grips with their hopes and aspirations, the Black community soured and the expressions of protest became physical rather than just verbal. For years the Black community strained every nerve to catch a sound from the President in favor of strong, effective, and enforceable civil rights. It listened in vain. There were always platitudes and testimonies of faith in the future and faraway reasoning, but nothing more.

Back in 1952 on the Campaign Train, the President had talked to me about his limited experience with Blacks, as well as his assignment after West Point with a Negro National Guard Regiment, the old 8th Illinois.

The young, sharp, highly trained "Pointer" was disappointed in the awkwardness, lack of education and interest of the outfit. In contests on rifle ranges and in other competitions with white outfits, they fared not too well. This kind of association at an early and impressionable age probably grooved the President's thinking.

During World War II he heard reports on Black outfits through his commanding generals, many of them southerners and irreconcilable rebels on the question of race and color. To those of us who participated in the war, the role of the Black soldier was tough. Often friendless and occasionally leaderless, his sorry record could be attributed to inferior leadership on the part of indifferent and inept white officers.

Many of the President's intimate friends and constant companions were from the deep South. For example, George Allen, a close friend of the President, never spoke to me despite the fact that we were thrown together several times. Likewise, the great amount of time spent in Augusta, Georgia, and in visiting various plantations of friends undoubtedly had at least an indirect influence upon the President's attitude. This is the negative side.

Conversely, there is much to be said for what Blacks achieved under the Eisenhower administration. The gains are impressive when viewed objectively. For example, Washington was desegregated—schools and all. This was done quietly and effectively after the President stated that he wanted the District of Columbia to be a model city. His staff passed the word to the city leaders of business and politics and the job was done almost overnight. It is only fair to say that the spectacular victory by Blacks in the Thompson Restaurant cases augured defeat for the diehards. But Ike's firmness completed the job.

Although desegregation of the Armed Forces started under President Truman, the services dragged their feet and demurred. Dwight Eisenhower gave a firm order and set a time limit and the segregated walls of the Armed Forces came tumbling down. This was a sizable victory.

The President also made some notable "first" Black appointments. Among them were: Chairman, Federal Parole Board; Assistant Secretary of Labor; Administrative Assistant in the White House; Private Secretary in the White House; Assistant to the Ambassador to the United Nations; Assistant to the Assistant Postmaster General; Regional Directors, I.C.A.; Ambassador to Guinea; Minister to Romania; Major General in the Air Force; and Members of Battle Monuments Commission. Many Negroes were upgraded in government service.

There is one odd observation to be made about these appointments: they indicated a new spirit and attitude in the Executive Branch. However, when J. Ernest Wilkins, Assistant Secretary of Labor, resigned, no Black took his place. The same thing happened with regard to the Parole Board, the governorship of the Virgin Islands, the secretary in the White House, and the Register of the Treasury. Thus, we ended up with fewer jobs than when we began.

I agree with the reasoning behind not refilling some of these jobs with Black candidates. This prevented the positions from being labeled "Negro jobs." But the general feeling was that comparable appointments should have been made.

Let no one say that Dwight Eisenhower did not have a heavy heart and troubled mind over the plight of Blacks in the United States. He could not escape it. The rising tide of color all over the world merely accentuated the deficiencies here at home. He firmly believed that people's hearts had to change before any change could come, and he did not believe one changed hearts by law or fiat. So his solution added up to a long and faraway timetable. This Blacks were unable and unwilling to abide.

After my job-hunting became a cause célèbre, the President mentioned it at a Cabinet meeting. He stated in effect that all was not well in a nation where one of his staff, because of color, was denied suitable job opportunities.

It is likewise significant that on the night he spoke on the Ellipse at the national Christmas lighting ceremony, his theme was that of our inhumanity to each other. He called for a better America where neither color, race, nor creed would deny one the right to earn a living in a job commensurate with training, skills, and background.

How do you explain this in view of his record of failure to take a strong moral leadership or to use the persuasive power of his office in the field of civil and human rights? The partial answer is: He knew me. I was a member of his official family and had served him loyally and (according to his letters) well. He could not extend this fellowship and concern to the masses. Thus, Dwight David Eisenhower missed an immortal place beside Lincoln in the hearts of Black Americans. They felt he let them down badly at a critical time in their period of national development.

THE FINAL MONTH AT THE WHITE HOUSE DECEMBER 1960—JANUARY 1961

After the November defeat at the polls, the mood at the White House was somber and gloomy. Staff members who had dreams of remaining in Washington with the Nixon Administration were scrambling now to find new jobs.

An office had been established at the White House to help staffers in their job-hunting. The government agencies were being combed to find unfilled slots, but the pickings in government were lean. Also, "to the victor belongs the spoils," and the new Democratic administration would soon be on the scene to dispossess all job-holders not covered by civil service.

The Republican giants of industry were cooperating to help the more prominent members of the staff land good spots. Several had already left even before the November debacle and were ensconced in cushy jobs in banks, Wall Street law firms, or Fortune 500 corporations.

I had to face my own problem of new employment alone. The White House office informed me in the middle of December that it could not locate anything for me. On my own, I had written and visited over twenty firms throughout the East and Middle West, but none of them could offer me anything at that time.

It was a frightening period for me and I was completely devastated by the inability of wealthy corporate members of the inner White House circle to aid me. Nelson Rockefeller sent me to see his Dartmouth classmate, Victor Borella, the director of Rockefeller Center, for possible assistance. He turned me down cold! I went to six or seven more of the same group and they all expressed regrets.

Five days before Christmas, President Eisenhower held his annual Christmas gathering for his staff. We gathered on the ground floor of the White House for coffee and cake and to receive a gift from the President and Mrs. Eisenhower. The gift was usually a replica of one of his paintings and a beautiful Christmas card signed by both the President and Mrs. Eisenhower. They are cherished gifts.

The President circulated around the room greeting each person. When he reached me, he gave a hearty hello to my staff and turned to me and said: "Fred, come with me for a minute." We walked along the hall and entered a small room with a lighted fireplace. It was the room President Roosevelt had used for his famous "fireside chats" with the nation in the critical depression years of the 1930s.

We stood facing each other near the fireplace and the President began to speak: "Fred, it is difficult for me to tell you what I must say. It has worried me for some time and I hoped to effect a pleasant ending, but apparently that is not to be.

"I have canvassed all my personal friends and many prominent members of the party in an effort to get you a job. They all admit to your competence and ability, but they cannot offer you a job at the level you deserve. Apparently big business is not ready at this time to take a chance on Black employment in executive ranks.

"I had hoped that you and Gene Black (Chairman of the Board of Doubleday) could get together. He tells me he offered you a good job but that you turned it down because of the salary. That's too bad.

"You served me well and faithfully and it pains me to see you leave this House in this manner. I am truly sorry."

"Mr. President," I replied, "I am deeply appreciative of your personal efforts to help me. All my life I shall be eternally grateful to you for permitting me to serve you in the White House. I regret to state as firmly as I can that Mr. Black never made a firm offer to me and we never at any time discussed salary. The first appointment I had with him was a disaster because he was inebriated. His secretary and aide asked me to return on another date. I did. For a brief moment he held out a carrot to me but I never heard from him again.

"Sir, let me thank you again for your faith and your concern about my welfare." There were a few seconds of silence. As we shook hands, I saw tears in the corners of the President's eyes.

On December 22nd, two days after the President's party, press secretary Hagerty called me to say that Felix Belair, Jr. of *The New York Times* wanted to interview me. Jim said he approved if I wanted to go through with it. I agreed and Mr. Belair came to my office.

Belair opened by saying that he knew the nation would be interested in my plans for employment after January 20, 1961, and hoped I would give him the facts for a possible news story. Belair and I talked for an hour and the next day, December 23rd, the front page of the *Times* carried a two-column story, the contents of which went around the world! The principal papers everywhere at home and abroad carried the story or editorials. Even Tass, the Russian newsgathering agency, radioed a story to Moscow.

THE NEW YORK TIMES

* * *

Friday
December 23, 1960

PRESIDENT'S AIDE
FACES RACE BARS

Special Assistant Is Unable
to Find Industry Post
at Executive Level

By FELIX BELAIR, Jr.
Special to The New York Times.

WASHINGTON, Dec. 22—The first Negro to hold the position of Administrative Assistant to the President said today that "a jungle of racial barriers" had made it impossible for him to get an executive position in private industry.

E. Frederick Morrow, who has been a member of President Eisenhower's staff for the last five years, said his only offers of private employment after Jan. 20 were of a nature that "would confine me to working with the Negro community."

One such offer, from a Wall Street brokerage firm, would have doubled his present salary of $18,000 a year, he said.

"So it's not just a matter of money," said the 51-year-old lawyer, a graduate of Rutgers University Law School. "It still shocks a great many captains of industry when a Negro seeks a job on the executive level even though he dealt with them directly as part of his official White House assignment," he said.

Mr. Morrow has been the President's Administrative Assistant in Charge of Special Projects. A brother of Dr. John H. Morrow, American Ambassador to Guinea, he accompanied Vice President Nixon on his tour of Europe and Africa in 1957.

He served as a major in World War II. His search for private employment has taken him to twenty business and industrial concerns in the Middle West and East during the last year.

Admit Color Barrier

"But the story was always the same," he said today. "They all admit you have brains and ability and if it were not for your color, there would not be any barriers to hurdle in the business world."

Mr. Morrow said he was determined to hold out as long as possible against taking any employment—no matter how lucrative—that would limit him to dealing with other Negroes.

"When you spend a lifetime crashing the jungle of racial barriers and you achieve this kind of job, it's very dismaying to have to go back to the jungle," he said, and continued:

"Having made this break of being a complete American and doing a job that any American can do, I don't want to be in a position of restricted activity among a restricted segment of the American people."

He did not state his views because he felt sorry for himself, Mr. Morrow said, but "because it's a story that ought to be told."

"I'm a symbol of 20,000,000 people," he continued, "And I'm thinking about what it will do to them as well as what it does to me."

The White House aide recalled that his family had long been in the forefront of the fight for racial equality and that his sister was the first Negro teacher in New Jersey. The family home was in Hackensack.

U.S. RACISM
MOSCOW TASS RADIOTELETYPE IN ENGLISH TO EUROPE 0644 12/24 L

(Text) New York—"Eisenhower's Negro Aide Seeking A Job Finds Race Bar," *The New York Herald Tribune* reports today with a show of naivity. "The President's aide faces race bar—special assistant unable to find an industry post at executive level," *The New York Times* echoes.

Involved is Frederick [sic] Morrow, the first Negro in American history to be appointed administrative assistant to a U.S. President. Now that his duties as a member of Eisenhower's White House staff are coming to an end, Morrow offered his services to 20 American firms, but in vain! The "Jungle of Racial Barriers," as Felix Belair, *New York Times* correspondent reports, is making it impossible for him to obtain an executive position.

By appointing Morrow to the first administrative position held by a Negro, the White House reckoned on misleading public opinion and creating the impression that racism in the United States is a thing of the past. Morrow's suffering has dispelled the publicity fog and revealed the true face of America's racial reality. Morrow declared: "It is a story that should be told. I am a symbol of 20 million people."
FBIS 12/24 324A PAK/HM

Chapter Thirty-two

Four days before the inauguration of President John F. Kennedy on January 20, 1961, I bade farewell to the White House and walked from those hallowed grounds into a dark and unknown void—jobless, dispirited, and without hope.

A few days before, a contingent of prominent Democrats had visited me in my home to make an offer. They said they appreciated my efforts to break new ground in the fight for human and civil rights and they felt I had conducted myself courageously and honestly. The new administration could use my expertise and general knowledge about Washington's political battleground. If I would just denounce and renounce the Republican Party and join the Democratic banner, a good, well-paying job would be available.

I was not flattered. I was livid! However, as a good host should, I proffered another round of drinks and spoke thusly:

"For almost eight years in this town, I worked for and

pledged allegiance to a Republican president. I spoke all over the nation espousing his policies and program. I accepted his defeats as part of my job, and I gloried in his victories because of my own input. The Republican Party has many flaws. Much of its philosophy is the philosophy that characterizes and depicts the thinking of most Americans. Its record on civil rights leaves much to be desired. Its interests in the problems of the poor and the downtrodden is slight. It is the party of the powerful and the rich. It is counter to many of the values included in my own personal code for living. Because of all these lacks, it needs some Blacks with guts, courage, and toughness to stay in it and fight like hell for reforms and changes.

"It is so easy to be a Democrat! The party stands for all the things that the underprivileged and the denied aspire to and for. It has the support of labor and other organized groups. It also has an irreconcilable southern wing that is thoroughly anti-Negro and almost anti-Christian. It has its share of bigots and racists and spoilers. So how do the scales of justice look when both parties are weighed in the balance? Mr. Kennedy cannot carry out his campaign promises that "with a stroke of the pen" he can change conditions in housing and other areas of civil rights. It can't be done! Trying to change the course of the old Ship of State is like trying to turn HMS Queen Elizabeth around in a narrow channel. It takes a lot of effort and a lot of time and a lot of years. And neither Democrats nor Republicans can or will do this until there is a change in the basic philosophy of white America on color and a wholesale national substitution of conscience for racism.

"For me to change parties for the gift of a job would be dishonest and contemptible. I would lose face with myself and all of Black America. I would be useless to you and to everybody else after eight years of carrying the ball for Dwight Eisenhower.

"Thank you and good night."

After leaving the White House, Catherine and I were ignored, rebuffed, and insulted by Blacks all across the country. They were saying: "You spent six years in the White House with that man and you never did a darn thing to get us out of the situation we're in . . ."

Thi kind of treatment and constant snide remarks were gettin us down. In my own mind, I had given my all, but appare tly no one knew it because it didn't show in what my critics elt were tangible ways. Racking my brain for a strategy I coul use to combat these accusations, I suddenly remembered he rough diary notes I had kept throughout those years. Somet mes at two or three in the morning, I would dictate a tape o what had happened during the day or week and my confid ntial secretary would transcribe them at home during her sp re time.

The e had been no plan devised ever to use these notes but my fri nds, the Alfred Moellers, who had given me the dictaphone urged the keeping of notes of events for posterity. I spent x months polishing the notes and developing them into book f rm with the title, *Black Man in the White House*.

I ca ed Doubleday, the publishers, and asked if they had any in erest in it. They said, "Of course! Anything about Eisenh wer interests us." They enthusiastically accepted the manus ipt. Six months passed, seven months, eight months, and no ing happened. I kept calling, and the only response I got was "it's still in committee."

Mari n Logan, an assistant at Doubleday, and incidentally a Black called me one day and said:

"Fre I have just insisted that they tell you the truth about your m nuscript. So tonight our vice president has consented to meet ou at the Sky-Top Club in Rockefeller Center for a cocktail o try to tell you—because nobody else will. He is a very dec nt, honorable man and he feels so badly about it that he will ake the responsibility of telling you exactly what happene 1."

So I m t the man and this is what he said: "Mr. Morrow, we were goi g to take the book and publish it. We planned to put money b hind it and it could have been a good seller. However, one day an Eisenhower aide and spokesman came in with the last d aft of the President's memoirs and we told him we were gett ng ready to publish your book. The spokesman said, 'If you pu blish anything that Fred Morrow writes, the President will withdraw his memoirs.'"

I could draw my own conclusions at that point. Doubleday had invested hundreds of thousands of dollars in Eisenhower's book and they were not about to foul up this contract under any circumstances.

There is an interesting sequel to this episode. I finally obtained the services of a top literary agent to market the book. He found that I had been blacklisted by all the principal publishers in America! Apparently, Republican friends of the President used their economic clout to stymie the publication and sale of my book.

The agent finally prevailed upon Coward-McCann to take the manuscript and publish it. It sold well both in hard cover and paperback and helped in a small degree to quell the erroneous and misplaced anger of many Negroes against my White House performance.

Today, *Black Man in the White House* is out of print and has become a collector's item. Libraries across the nation get constant calls for its use from graduate students in history or from historians writing about the Eisenhower period. My papers from the White House period are in the *E. Frederic Morrow Collection* at the Eisenhower Library in Abilene, Kansas; another collection, in the great library at Boston University, gets maximum use from writers and historians who are examining, under a microscope, the erratic history and progress of civil rights in America.

In 1964 President Eisenhower, from his farm in Gettysburg, decided to have a reunion of his cabinet, principal staff members, prominent appointees, and members of Congress. The purpose was to look at national issues and to assess what had to be done by the Republican Party to recapture the national scene.

I was invited to attend. It was to be an all-day meeting held at the posh hotel in Hershey, Pennsylvania, not too far from Gettysburg. We all arrived the evening before and had a splendid social time reminiscing and filling in the gaps. I found Milton Eisenhower particularly friendly and charming that night and he put at ease some of those who were surprised at my presence.

I didn't see the President until he arrived to open the morning meeting in a huge room equipped like a schoolroom with individual seats and desks for each attendee. I purposely sat in the back of the room, picking an end seat so that the others could have the option to move into the row or bypass it.

The President opened the meeting with a cheerful greeting and expressed pleasure at seeing all of his "old team."

We began the session by talking about what was wrong with the Party and why we lost the '60 election. After an hour of this, Claire Booth Luce said: "Mr. President, why don't we talk about Topic A?" She said, "The Black problem. Civil rights and the Blacks."

The President got kind of red and said: "Well, if you want to go at that, all right. That's vital. But let's stop and have a coffee break; we'll come back in fifteen minutes and we'll talk about Topic A."

I remained seated and did not join the pack drifting out for coffee. The President passed my desk as he went by, he stopped and said: "Fred, when we come back, I'm going to throw you to the dogs! Claire wants to talk about 'Topic A' and you were always ranting about this thing. Now you're here with the backbone of the party; so I'm going to throw you out there and you do whatever you want to do."

I was completely shaken up. I honestly didn't know what to do. My mind went blank and I started to perspire and feel weak. I hadn't come expecting anything like this; nor was I prepared either offensively or defensively to enter into an emotional debate on a subject Republicans tried to shun.

The audience returned. The President stood up on the platform and this is how he introduced me: "There is a man here today who I felt was my friend; but he wrote a book. I don't know whether he is my friend now or not. But I am going to let him get up here and tell you whatever he has on his mind; and you ask him anything you want. Fred Morrow."

The platform seemed like a mile away. There was no applause and I was very conscious of the almost hostile looks on the faces of many. "Mr. President," I said, "I am certain you have not read my book because if you had, you could not have introduced me the way you did this morning. I am devastated because in my book I bent over backwards, Sir, to let the world know what a great, honorable, decent man you are. And how together, we sweated blood to try to make this country a better place—not only for Negroes—but for everybody.

"I was the only person available to my race to bear their pitiful pleas for equal justice and opportunity. I was the only Administration office-holder they could hold guilty and responsible for the lackadaisical attitude of the Republican Party toward civil and human rights. They looked to me to nudge your elbow daily and guide you toward that last mile they've sought since the Proclamation of Emancipation.

"In their judgment I failed! And they have made my wife and me social pariahs in the Negro community of America.

"Mr. President, the only reason I wrote that book was to try to set the record straight and to let the world know that I had tried to serve decently and honorably my people and my country."

I sat down. The emotion in the room was intense. There was a standing ovation. After that episode, through the years until his death, I had some beautiful correspondence from the President. In each letter, it looked like he was trying to make amends for any former transgression. The walls of my study are lined with his tributes.

Any Black who has aspired beyond the cotton fields and the curbstones of America realizes that our very existence in this country since the cotton gin has been eased by a minority of courageous, earnest, fearless whites who champion the cause of equality of opportunity and justice for all humans irrespective of color, creed or social condition.

In every job and assignment I have ever had as an adult, these unsung disciples of justice have aided and abetted my will and determination to survive. Some were present in the White House and their character shone through in many crises. I am glad to list and comment on a few of them:

Anne Whitman, the President's personal secretary, was a noble woman as far as I knew. She had a feeling for the underprivileged. One of the reasons for whatever success I had in the White House was because Anne was the conduit for me to the President. She trusted my judgment. She felt if Fred Morrow had something he felt the President ought to see or know, she got it to him. She could issue little warnings about some of the "dogs" that might be after me because they didn't like my point of view. She had great responsibility and she also had great power. The personal secretary to the President of the United States is a very powerful person because she or he can make it tough for you to get in to see him. Or she can drop little things along the way that make it difficult when you get in there. Perhaps a lot of people didn't think too kindly of her because she was a sort of guard at the door, but she was able, efficient, loyal, and, above all, a regal lady.

General Andrew J. Goodpaster, Staff Secretary, was my friend and one of the finest human beings I have ever known. He was on my side. He was a favorite of the President. Andy was the kind of person who, when I was really in trouble or distress, would respond. He had a mind like a steel trap. A West Pointer, Princeton PhD., a brilliant and much decorated World War II veteran, he was the epitome of the best of American manhood.

James Hagerty, Press Secretary, was exceptional. He had remarkable instincts and he knew at a glance what the press would pursue relentlessly. He leveled with the media at all times, telling what he could honestly and completely, and indicating that what he had to withhold he would release when it was prudent to do so.

He never embarrassed the President either by a glib tongue, or personal conduct and his rating with his peers was "exceptional."

Black newsmen praised Hagerty for his empathy and fairness in dealing with the news and stories of particular interest to their readers and supporters.

I found him a decent, honest, honorable man and he did what he could to advance my cause.

William J. Hopkins, Executive Clerk, was honored by President Lyndon Johnson with the Public Service Medal. Hopkins was a calm, collected person with no flair. Nothing impressed him. He did his job; he was always there. Presidents have come and gone, but Hopkins was the permanent link in the government between administrations.

He knew everything: every niche and corner, the precedent for anything, and the protocol. He was one of the nation's truly great public servants and I really liked him. Bill never interfered with me, never made any overtures; but whenever I would test him, he stood up like a man. He wanted to see me make it because he felt it just had to be.

Gerald Morgan, Special Counsel to the President, was one of the first top staff members to extend the right hand of fellowship to me. On my first day of duty, he stepped forward to wish me well and to offer assistance if needed. He was a most able lawyer and prince of a man. Princeton- and Harvard-educated, he wore the badge of excellence well.

Socially, Gerry did a very significant thing for the Morrows. He invited us to a Sunday brunch at his country home in Maryland and among the guests were General and Mrs. Wilton Persons. We all got along and it was a beautiful occasion. It was a typical Morgan gesture. The Persons were his friends—so were the Morrows. What's the problem?

Chapter Thirty-three

The writing of this narrative finds me in the twilight of my life. If I had not lived every minute and incident reported, I would find it difficult to believe.

It seems incredulous and incredible that in the greatest civilized nation in the world, a citizen should find his color and race a hindrance and a barrier to a free and unhampered life, that decent housing, schooling, and employment (and even certain forms of recreation), should be beyond his ability to obtain. The scar-tissue from the fight for the simple basic needs of existence is thick around my soul. And years of striving to break down the barriers of denial by performing well within the system, have left me a "doubting Thomas" as to the wisdom of the effort.

I writhe in pain when I reflect upon the failure of America earnestly to observe the golden rule. As a nation, we give lip service and pious promises to the problems and needs of the underprivileged, but we continue to resist implementing actions to counteract these human ills. In writing this text, I referred to *Webster's New Collegiate Dictionary* for the definition of a "citizen." The dictionary definition is "One entitled to the rights and privileges of a free man."

That definition stings me to the quick. At seventy years of age I am still trying to acquire the simple civil rights embodied in my citizenship! This definition capsulizes the status of the millions of Blacks in this country. After more than three hundred years of residence, loyalty, effort and work, in bondage and out, Blacks are not full citizens of this nation. Full citizens do not have to fight for civil rights!

With this half-status, we find ourselves between a rock and a hard place. It is obvious that our presence in America continues to disturb the white race. We are no longer needed to serve the great plantations of the South, or to hew wood or carry water anywhere in the land. Machines do that now. So, devoid of education and opportunity to survive in a technical environment, we stand on the street corners of the land and contemplate revenge. We cannot be exiled; we cannot be accommodated; we cannot rebel. So what do we do?

In 1968 the National Advisory Commission on Civil Disorders, rendered a report, a paragraph of which I quote here:

> This is our basic conclusion. Our nation is moving toward two societies, one white and one black—separate and unequal . . . the most fundamental [cause of riots] . . . is the racial attitude and behavior of white America toward Black Americans. . . . Race prejudice has shaped our history decisively; it now threatens to affect our future. . . . White racism is essentially responsible for the explosive mixture which has been accumulating in our cities since the end of World War II. . . .

I shudder for my country when I think of her future headaches and tragedies. America's refusal to understand and solve its race problem leaves it ill-equipped to help in solving the problems of the Middle East, or South America, or Africa.

I have a strong spiritual feeling that within the next decade, there will develop in America a strong crusade to solidify and preserve democratic government and life, as the cries and the pressures for full citizenship *for all Americans* demand changes in our present farcical and lukewarm performance.

In America's race with the Soviets for the acquisition of the minds and loyalty of peoples to preserve our political way of life, our nation will have to deal forthrightly with the problem of color and race. With the United Nations located in the United States, and daily viewing (and sometimes victims of) our nation's attitude on color and race, we will have to eliminate this moral weakness or relinquish any semblance of leadership in the free world.

Sometime ago I attended a Bat Mitzvah in a Westchester synagogue. This is the female version of the Bar Mitzvah. The young lady, daughter of a valued friend, was being inducted into Jewish adult society. The ceremony was solemn and gripping. Centuries old, the music and the scriptures cried out the sorrow and tragedy of an eternity of inhumanity. The young rabbi, in a ten minute sermon, impressed upon the youth that this ceremony is over 3,000 years old. He called her to begin a life of service to her God and her people. It signaled the fact that she had reached the age of human concern. He said Jews had survived for 3,000 years with only the ten commandments as basic law for living—and without police or courts or soldiers to compel Jews' loyalty to kin, they had survived, prospered, and persevered for thirty centuries.

I left the ceremony deeply moved. It was inevitable that I would compare the situation of these people with that of my own. Blacks were slaves—driven from pillar to post—ravaged, maimed, degraded and killed—we still survive, three hundred years later in an almost alien land. On balance we have done well merely to survive—but with all our experiences we have neither learned nor achieved the cohesiveness, race pride, and determination to overcome all the barriers erected to prevent our induction into the society of first-class citizenship.

A token group has viewed the "promised land," but the great masses in America still stand in the four corners of the land and cry out against injustice and deprivation. The brief "era of good feeling" induced by Martin Luther King's courage and self sacrifice, is past and almost forgotten. The Klan is riding again. Race relations have reached an impasse; despite the Supreme Court, after twenty-five years, segregation in the schools still exists and efforts to integrate the educational system are blocked at every point. Black admissions are diminishing in our professional schools—and the job market is frozen—despite the few hundred token jobs played up in the press as "breakthrough" on big time. The "cop-out"—the dropout problem—among our youth is startling and overwhelming. The drug culture has enrolled thousands of our young, and the jails and prisons are bursting at the seams with Black inmates. The President of the United States has upbraided us for not registering and voting and yet we are griping about the way we are treated by the political parties of our country.

Economically, we are still the tail of the financial dog in America and despite our ninety-billion-dollar potential we still pay for what we want and beg for what we need!

I've decided to make a pitch for the beginning of a crusade that will forever free us from pursuing the tinsel and froth of life which for many years has prevented us from reaching the place for which our parents sighed. I will attempt to outline some of our responsibilities in this current crisis of hardened race relations in this country, and will completely ignore how far we have come down the rugged road of time, in order to point out how far we have to go to reach the promised land of full citizenship. First-class citizenship means severe responsibilities as well as refreshing privileges. The privileges are easy to accept; the responsibilities can be bitter and odious to acknowledge.

For over three centuries, we have been seeking the right to be estimated like white Americans, by a single yardstick of evaluation. We abhor and despise the double standard which for us means denial. So what we have been saying since the fifties in our sit-ins, our kneel-ins, our wade-ins, and our regional invasions, is that we are now ready to be evaluated on the same basis, by the same standards, with the same rules, and with the same demands, as other Americans. This is fine. This gives the fight meaning, and makes the sacrifices sensible and meritorious. But isn't there another step?

Somewhere in this blueprint for freedom must be instructions on how we prepare to accept and wear the grave obligations and responsibilities that will come to us with our hard-won victory.

Thirty years ago, I applied to a big commercial firm in New Jersey for an executive position. At an interview grudgingly given by the president of the firm, he asked me to tell him some important facts about myself. I was proud and perhaps impressed by the fact that the recently published book, *Who's Who in Colored America*, carried my biography. I related this fact. My interviewer said to me cold-bloodedly—"That's unimportant and unimpressive. The day you make *Who's Who in America*, come back and see me!" This was a brutal reply, but it contained a valuable lesson: white America is responsive only to the standards it has developed and codified as the sine qua non. No matter what accolades a non-white might recieve from his race, tribe, or family, they cannot be traded for the greatest badge of all—equality.

Through three centuries Blacks have been competing mostly against each other for acceptance. We were born into, lived, worked, and competed in a Black world. Standards were evolved and set for us that were good and noble, but had neither the authority nor the authenticity of those set for the majority community. Through our history a handful of Blacks has had both the courage and the ability to engage in hand to hand combat with the white man's standards of achievement, and despite the odds and the super discouragements, win a signal and meaningful victory. But for the vast majority, the horizon has been limited to the Black world.

So, in the shape of things to come, none of us in any avenue of life, will be competing solely against other Blacks with separate rules to determine the winners. From this point on, each one of us will be competing against the best this nation has to offer and survival of the fittest will be the acid and only test.

So all responsible organizations and groups have the important duty of warning Blacks about the frightening and stubborn problems at hand, and the obligation to develop plans and avenues of training to prepare our youth (and the not too old) for the realities of today.

Whether we accept the fact or not, we are now engulfed in the frenzied struggle of our race to eliminate the last barriers to self-respect and complete social and economic acceptance. We have a choice. The achievers can sit on their hands and let the zealous—but not necessarily knowledgeable—persons do the job; or, they can join in and attempt to give leadership and direction to a crusade that will determine forever our status in the United States.

One of the dangers in an emotional period like this is that it offers fertile ground for the rise of false prophets and self-annointed leaders. In so many cities today, anyone who leads a picket line, makes a flamboyant public statement, resists the status quo, or forms a cult to overthrow anything, is deemed and unblushingly called "a leader." It is the perfect setting for the emergence of scoundrels and dead beats who have nothing but color in common with our legitimate aims and aspirations. We must continually be on the lookout for, and warn against, these charlatans.

Another critical area for development and readjustment is our youth. The whole purpose of this struggle is lost if our youth do not share the purpose of the crusade as well as the desired results. I say this with full knowledge that it was our youth in the fifties who lit the spark as well as made the greatest sacrifices to set off the crusade. But even while they were fighting and dying for a cause so noble and just, they did not fully realize that with victory would come new and greater demands upon their courage and faith and stamina.

We must say to our youth that with the end of segregation, and with the adoption of the rule of one standard of evaluation for determining who belongs and who is rewarded, the old cry of failure because of color, cannot be used to cover up for ineptitude or lack of preparation. May the Good Lord speed the day when the crutch of color will no longer serve to support the ill-equipped, the ill-prepared, or the lazy!

The appalling number of dropouts among Black grammar and high school students is most alarming. It is one of the stumbling blocks in the way to successful acceptance in every facet of American life. I can understand the discouragements, problems, denials, poverty, and hopelessness that cause many to leave school before the rudimentary elements of an education are acquired. With the present so bleak and hopeless, it appears to these youth absurd to be concerned about the challenges and the claims of the future. Somehow we must get the message across to them as quickly as possible that within the next five years or so, a person without at least a high school education, will be an unemployed person, and perhaps a perpetual case for charity. This world of science and automation in which we live will not be kind or responsive to those who cannot perform tasks evolving from the machines and situations they create. Being engaged in a movement designed to give us freedom and self-respect does not give us license to be crude or rude or impertinent to other people. Poverty and denial are horrible enemies of tranquility and equilibrium. However, they cannot be overcome by plundering, murdering, or maiming. As long as the jails and the penal institutions of the nation hold an abnormal percentage of Blacks within their walls, we cannot shake the stigma of a disregard for the tenets of law, order, and civility.

I would like to see the NAACP, the Urban League, the churches and schools start a drive to make young people conscious of the absolute necessity of mastering the English language. As one moves about the streets in the cities of this country, one is amazed and stung by the jargon and the "jive" that children use to transmit ideas and thoughts. It is at best a crude tribal tongue and it is one more thing to make us stick out like a sore thumb, making the problem of acceptance more difficult and impossible.

During my days in the White House, more than 50 percent of the Blacks who were turned down for jobs or promotions in governmental agencies and institutions were turned down because they could neither speak nor write satisfactory English. Some of them would appeal to me for help, and often I could not translate what they were trying to say.

In this drive for recognition as equals, an enormous amount of race pride and a knowledge of race history are required. One of the tragedies of segregation is that we by necessity study from the books of our oppressors which deny our identity and worth. Unless we come from homes where time and patience were taken to impress upon our minds the contributions of our ancestries to the glory and the grandeur of America or from good Negro schools where the teaching of race pride and achievement were part of the curricula, we will grow up with a sterile and hopeless feeling of a lack of identity with anything worthwhile or consequential. Too few youth today know the names of Frederick Douglass, Booker T. Washington, Sojourner Truth, or William B. DuBois. These are but a few of the heroes and heroines who hacked a niche for themselves and lit a flame of hope for their race out of the bleak offerings of a cruelly segregated and uncharitable era.

Again, I would like to see the churches and fraternal groups take the lead in debunking the idea that the acquisition of "things," is an acceptable substitute for qualities of character, intelligence, training, and a durable sense of values to live by. More often than not today we see our friends and acquaintances hurtling pell-mell after the tinsel and froth of life, ignoring the substance and the real. As a result, I have heard some of our young people in awed envy, resolve that they, too, at the earliest possible moment, will set out to acquire the "things" that give an aura of success to those who collect them.

When we put a $45 hat on a nickel head, we fool no one but ourselves. And this rule is true in any transaction where we ignore the laws of economics in favor of the foolish, frilly whims of fancy.

In 1955, in a speech to the Elks Convention held in Atlantic City, I made a plea for Blacks to stop paying for what they want, and begging for what they need. I also suggested that, out of the 15 billion dollar income then available to us, that we support such organizations as the NAACP, the Urban League, and the Community Chest—rather than spending 3 billion a year on whiskey, furs, cars, and other gew-gaws of life.

After that speech, the din from the Black community was terrific! Sacks of inflammatory mail came to the White House denouncing me as a "traitor to the race," "the white man's tool," and "a fool with a job too big for him." A national group made representation to the President to fire me at once and editorials in the Black press roasted me with invective and disdain. It took me a long time to recover from that assault.

233

But happily today one can see the philosophy expounded in that speech accepted as the sine qua non of the Freedom Movement; and any Black fraternity, sorority, social or fraternal order worth its salt is contributing time, money, and effort to the big cause for the common good. The March on Washington eight years later proved that we had arrived at a stock-taking time. Unless we were willing to pay the cost for the job, we were doomed to failure.

This effort is challenging and compelling in part because the paths we must cross on our way to freedom have never been charted nor marked for us. No Black has ever seen "Freedomland" and so the way is tricky and devious and laden with pitfalls and landslides. Our only guides and assets are deep and abiding courage, an eternal faith that we are right and ordained by God to walk this land in dignity and in peace.

In his message to the Congress on February 28, 1963, President Kennedy said, "The Negro baby born in America today—regardless of the section or state in which he is born—has about one-half as much chance of completing high school as a white baby born in the same place on the same day—one-third as much chance of becoming a professional man—twice as much chance of becoming unemployed—about one-seventh as much chance of earning $10,000 per year—a life expectancy which is seven years less—and the prospects of earning only half as much." In 1979, the odds have multiplied by ten. Who among us in this struggle, or even outside of it can fail to be shaken and concerned by this picture of the blighted hopes and dreams of generations yet to come?

No American, white or Black, can escape the clamor of the outside world today, where the common folk are demanding that each and every human being should have the privilege to determine his or her right to enjoy a free and untrammeled life on earth. I hope every reader of this book will feel some sense of responsibility toward nudging our country toward a posture more compelling and inspiring than a dateline commemorating our historic inhumanity.

Despite the bitter memories and heartbreak of the past, I shall not turn back, nor sit in a corner and sulk away my remaining days. I remain a true believer that, with God's help, we shall overcome someday, someday. But I have equal convictions that we have deep obligations and hard decisions to make and tests to achieve if the sacrifices of Martin Luther King, Jr., Medgar Evars, and a host of others who died for our cause are to bear fruit and make us totally free citizens in this nation, now and for all times.

This means that, with every living day, we must pursue, absorb, and produce the best in every endeavor that comes to our hands to do. We must resolve that, God being our witness, we shall never turn or look back in despair, shrink in courage, or balk at death in carrying out these sacred obligations to ourselves and our fellows.